Managing Yourself

Managing Yourself

Mike Pedler and Tom Boydell

Gower

Published in association with Fontana Paperbacks by
Gower Publishing Company Limited
Gower House
Croft Road
Aldershot
Hants GU11 3HR
England

British Library Cataloguing in Publication Data
Pedler, Mike *1944–*
  Managing yourself.
  1. Business enterprise. Success
  I. Title II. Boydell, Tom *1940*
  650.1

ISBN 0 566 02851 4

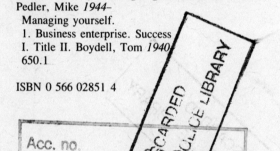
Printed in Great Britain by
Billing & Sons Ltd, Worcester

Contents

Preface

This book is intended for 'the thinking manager'. That's not to say that it is all theoretical — far from it. After all, managing is above all about getting things done.

However, we are now, towards the end of the twentieth century, on the edge of what is sometimes called the 'New Age' — an era in which old ways of doing things, of managing 'by the seat of the pants', will no longer be appropriate. This book is intended for managers who are aware that times are changing, who are becoming conscious of:

- the need to unblock people and organizations, to release them from the grips of bureaucracy and/or blind, unthinking, inhuman commitment to 'the bottom line'
- the need to empower individuals so that they can shake off their dependency on increasingly inexpert experts, so that they can instead develop their own expertise
- their desire to unleash the pent-up creative energies within people and organizations that at present go unrecognized, unrewarded, unwanted
- the need to consider the whole person; to manage ideas, feelings, and actions; to work with the physical, mental and spiritual parts of ourselves
- the way things are connected, so that you just *cannot* try to ignore other people, or other parts of the organization, or other parts of the world, pretending that these do not exist and/or are enemies to be defeated
- the imbalances in the world with regard to the distribution of food, power and freedom and all the other aspects of human society, and yet ...

- . . . the growing sense that we are 'one world'; part of a connected whole
- the rate of technical change, growing at a phenomenal rate, and the rate of growth of information available to managers, which is growing even faster
- the fact that fundamental relationships between 'work'/'leisure', 'employment'/'unemployment' are being challenged and reassessed
- the fact that although in some ways 'managing' is simple, it is also very complex; and, in particular, simplistic solutions to our problems, bags of tricks and gimmicks, while appearing attractive, are in reality nothing more than an illusion

In this book we state a number of our beliefs about the person the New Age manager will have to be. Certainly, she or he will have to be able to combine *both* doing *and* thinking. Thus, I will take action in full awareness of what I am doing, of why, and of what its consequences might be for me, for others, for my organization and for the environment.

Only when I am working in this way can I be said really to be managing myself. It is another of our beliefs that you cannot manage others unless you are able to manage yourself – to be proactive, rather than allowing yourself to be buffeted and controlled by events and other people. So this book is about working from the inside out; from managing myself to managing the world around me.

The process of the book

In keeping with our belief in combining thought and action, we have set out to do that in the way we have written this book. We have tried to make it active by going through a process of exploring various aspects of managing yourself. This involves:

- warming up to the subject; developing an interest in it
- shedding light on it; analysing, looking in depth
- weighing things up; deciding what it means for you in terms of action

● grounding, or carrying out the action, and then reviewing what you have done

We have done this in a variety of ways. You will find a number of 'warming-up' questionnaires and case studies, to start you thinking. Then we explore and analyse a number of aspects of self-management. And then there are activities/exercises that you can do to improve and develop the way you manage yourself.

Perhaps it will be useful to make a couple of points here. First, we are not suggesting that you should attempt to carry out all the exercises in one fell swoop. What we are suggesting is that you concentrate, in the first instance, on a few activities that for one reason or another appeal to you. You can always come back to some of the others later. Also you will find that virtually all the activities are such that they can be repeated from time to time. Doing them just once, and then assuming that that's it for all time, is as silly as saying, 'I went to the cinema once, so there's no point going again.'

Indeed, some of the activities won't work at all *unless* they are carried out regularly. After all, you can't expect to get physically fit simply by going for one two-mile run. You need gradually to build up a regime of exercise, appropriate to you, your needs, your starting level and your goal. And the same is true of many of the practical things that we describe here.

We have also tried to write the book in a way that involves you, and relates to your own experience, while requiring that you engage in active consideration of these new perspectives on managing. Self-management is basically a self-empowering process, and one of the powers we hope to develop is that by which you may find your own knowledge, rather than merely relying on receiving knowledge from others.

Hopefully we are breaking new ground here – that may, in parts, surprise you, challenging, as it does, some of the earlier ideas about management that are no longer good enough in these times of change. So, for all these reasons, approach this book with an open mind. Above all, don't believe anything we say. Work with it, and come to your own conclusions.

The structure of the book

We look at the question of managing oneself in more depth in Chapter 1, working with various models of self-management. Then, in Chapters 2 to 6, we explore these aspects in turn in more detail, starting with the planning and carrying out of *action* in Chapter 2.

Chapters 3 and 4 then look at *knowing, valuing* and *being* yourself, followed by managing yourself and your skills (Chapter 5) and your health (Chapter 6).

We then move further outwards from the self. It is clear that in order to learn to manage ourselves properly, we need other people, to challenge and support us. We look at this in some detail in Chapter 7. Similarly, you manage yourself within some organizational context, so Chapter 8 is devoted to organizational considerations.

Chapter 9 is at once the easiest and most difficult; the most important and and least important; the simplest and the most complex; the most obvious and the most subtle; the shortest and the longest; the one you should read before the others, and the one that should not be read until after the rest. 'The most important things about managing myself.'

Finally, Chapter 10 provides some jumping off points to take you on with your self-development. Here you will find some recommended books on managing yourself, managing others and managing in the organization, each with a brief description of the contents. All these books have been chosen to be 'reader friendly'. At the end of this section are a few useful addresses of organizations concerned with management education and development who will provide information courses, newsletters and other services.

Mike Pedler
Tom Boydell

1 Managing yourself

MANAGING ME FIRST

The fundamental assumption behind this book is that anyone who wants to improve the way they manage others must first learn to manage themselves. If we can create order in ourselves then we have taken the first step to creating order amongst others and in the environment in which we work. Thus, we need to learn to manage from the inside out, starting with managing yourself (i.e., *managing me*) and then moving out to managing the people and world around us. So let's make a start by looking at how well you are managing yourself.

INSIDE/OUTSIDE

As a starter activity, try thinking about the way you are managing yourself and your environment. Jot down on a piece of paper – or in a special 'Self-management Logbook' – four or five occasions when you feel you managed something or somebody really well. And then the same for when you did it pretty badly. Now, for each of those occasions, can you recall how you were in yourself? Were you fully in control, doing what you wanted, saying just what you intended to say, handling your feelings rather than allowing them to overwhelm you? Or were you out of control, losing your temper, not able to express yourself properly, failing to find the right words that you knew were there somewhere but couldn't get hold of?

11

There will probably be a link between these events. When you *were* in control, in charge, consciously managing yourself, that's when things went well. And when you lost control of yourself, that's when you lost control of the situation.

In other words, managing from the inside out rests upon the idea that what is outside us is a reflection of what is inside us, and vice versa. This suggests that the way I carry out my formal managerial role is likely to be based upon the way I manage myself and my immediate environment. I cannot really manage things outside of me until I can manage my inner self. Conversely, I cannot really manage myself until I can manage my outer world.

That is the basic message of this book. We can show it diagrammatically, as in Figure 1.1.

Before going any further, let's look at how it is for you.

HOW IT IS FOR ME

Looking at Figure 1.1, consider you and your world. Write down what seems to be going well, because of you, in each of the circles. What's good about the way you're managing yourself – what are you doing with and for your abilities, skills, talents, physical and mental condition that please you? Next, what's good about the way you're managing people and things immediately around you – at work and at home?

Then to the next ring: what's going well in your department or area of activity because of you? And finally, what of the outer ring? Can you say that you are making any contribution to your community – what are you putting into it, how are you helping to manage it?

Now the other side of the coin. What's not so good in each of those circles? In what ways are you not doing such a good job of managing them? What pressures, worries, unresolved issues are you aware of?

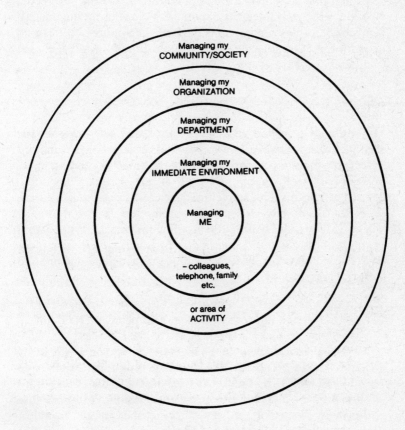

Figure 1.1 *Managing from the inside out*

It's almost certainly true that in your life there are some aspects, in each ring, that you are managing well, and others that you are managing badly. If you can't think of any in the 'doing well' category, this is probably because you are making a poor job of managing your self-image; you are failing – or refusing – to recognize and value your talents. Chapter 4 looks at this in some detail. Conversely, if everything seems perfect, then either you have no need for this book, or you are a bit short on self-knowledge – see Chapter 3.

Peter Ford: a short case study

You are your own best case study; that's why we suggested the above exercise. However, we can look at other people's situations to form the basis of comparisons, and to use as a 'worked example' in other parts of the book. So here's an extract from a day in the life of Peter Ford, a personnel manager at a large bank. Peter is thirty-nine, and has climbed the promotion ladder unusually quickly. Many of his colleagues envy him his success, his apparent energy and his obvious commitment; he is earmarked for a place on the board in two or three years' time – although no one has told him so. Now read on:

8.30 a.m.: Peter arrives at his office, fifteen minutes earlier than usual but fifteen minutes later than he'd planned. He'd got up at 7.00 a.m. to make it to the office to clear his desk, but he'd had a heavy social evening the night before and he was scarcely warmed up by his tea and toast and largely automatic exchanges with the family. The traffic had been just as bad as it was at his normal time – and all those green notes waiting for him before the main events of the day! Peter dashes up to his floor, nodding 'hello' to the Head of Foreign in the lobby, but failing to notice the greeting of the commissionaire, and all the time hoping that he won't meet any of his colleagues who will no doubt want to engage him in social chit chat. . . .

1.30 p.m.: lunch. In the half hour available before meeting

his fellow personnel managers to discuss a contentious incentive scheme to promote manager mobility in the bank, Peter eats a sandwich and sips coffee while working through those remaining green notes. After long practice he can hold the telephone between his left shoulder and cheek while writing answers to memos, letters etc. That's one of the reasons he has been successful in getting so much done – compared with some of his colleagues he seems able to cram twelve hours of work into a ten-hour day. The morning had disappeared under the assault of three meetings. The one at 9.00 a.m. to agree the new job description for the Community Projects Officers dragged on for two hours thanks to Ken Wallington's tedious nit-picking. At the end of this meeting Peter already had a headache. The next meeting with Pam Walton and John Novarra had been more fun and Peter had been sorry when he'd had to rush off to attend his boss's weekly briefing.

He stopped writing for a moment, put down the phone and massaged the left side of his neck. Bloody rheumatism, no doubt. He thought about the rest of the day – more meetings, at least two hours of letter-writing, reading and corrections, and then off to catch the shuttle to Edinburgh for tonight's dinner and tomorrow's training conference. Not much time for relaxation there, and probably more food and drink than was good for him. It'll be even worse next week in Paris – the price of success!

Momentarily Peter felt sorry for himself. Why did he always take on too much? Why hadn't he said 'No' to that conference? He knew the answer to this one – it was his own need to keep tabs on everything, to know what was going on, and to keep himself in the limelight.

So much of his life was like this now. Not only was the job more demanding and complex, but you seemed to have to spend more and more time politicking to stay up with the field. Actually, when he thought about it, Peter didn't like that part of himself very much. He could fight and struggle for power and resources along with the rest of the 'streetfighters' at head office, but did he want to live like this? He could do without the snidery and aggression, the calculation and the secrecy. . . .

And on the rare occasions when he stopped to think about it, he had a nagging feeling that a lot of what he did was not all that important anyway, it was all self-generated. What was it achieving – for himself or for anyone else? In what way could the world be said to be a better place because of him? Sometimes the thought of spending another twenty-five years doing this was . . . well, it sent a shudder through him.

Other people didn't put in the hours he did. . . . And then the human contact was not all it could be. You were always pushing, chasing people for work and so on. Surely you should have time to relax, to make jokes, to have fun . . .?

. . . And, he concluded, the kids were growing up fast and without a lot of help from him. Since Pat had returned to work and got interested in her own career, the times when they coincided in giving their full attention to each other were few and far between. . . .

2.00 p.m.: Peter dumps his cup and sandwich wrapper in the bin, puts on his jacket, picks up his pen, diary and note pad, and heads for room 202. . . .

Okay. You get the picture. Peter Ford is in many ways a successful manager and yet his life is in a mess. He's not the only one of us to be on a treadmill powered partly by our own inner compulsions and partly by the demands of all those others in our life – colleagues, boss, customers, clients . . . even making time for friends and family feels like another pressure. If Peter doesn't stop himself soon, something else probably will. Yet how can he break out of this state, this man-made mould, this patiently accumulated self-image?

And how much of Peter do you see in yourself? After all, it's one thing to see from the outside; to notice the mistakes and traps that this fictional manager is falling into (although notice that his colleagues had quite a different view of him. What did his wife and family think?). So how well can you see yourself? How good a job

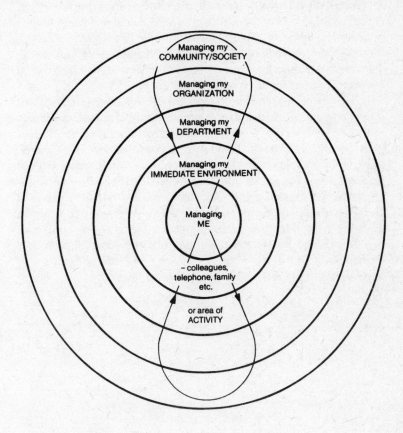

Figure 1.2 *Managing from the inside out*

are you doing at managing both yourself *and* the world around you?

This process is one of flowing out from yourself, into contact with others and with your environment, giving to them, and thus receiving and learning in turn, hence flowing back into yourself, changing and developing inwards as well as outwards, managing both inner and outer. To emphasize this we can superimpose this 'double-loop' of learning on the earlier diagram, as in Figure 1.2. The arrows show that this is a continuous, dynamic flow of movement, from inner to outer to inner, etc.

In fact, we can take this a step further. We have talked of our inner and outer worlds, and have stressed that these are inextricably linked. If we take the loop out from Figure 1.2 and redraw it on its own, then which part of this loop is the most important? Clearly, you cannot say that either of them is. The loop cannot exist without both parts – just as you cannot have a one-sided coin. This apparently simple notion has enormous significance; it is an example of changing from thinking in terms of 'either —— or ——' (i.e. 'either the inner or the outer is the most important') to 'both —— and ——' (i.e., 'both the inner and the outer are the most important'.) Perhaps we can call it *synergistic thinking* – i.e. thinking in a way that brings things together, rather than polarizing them.

INNER   OUTER

Figure 1.3

This change to synergistic thinking – moving away from 'either —— or ——' to 'both —— and ——' – has profound implications. For example, take the question of management development. In

18

the past, this has very largely concentrated on the outer world, focusing on models and theories of economics, business, market places, etc. Even when learning about people, the emphasis is almost entirely on *other* people, what motivates *them*, what makes *them* tick, etc. How many management courses give syllabus space to areas like '*my*self; *my* motivations; what makes *me* tick; how *I* behave as a consumer'?

Not only does the content of management education focus almost entirely on the outside world, but so does its process. Nearly all the teaching of managing assumes that we learn by being force-fed a diet of predigested knowledge and distilled wisdom from the past.

This is a conservative tradition that in fact hinders our learning about managing, by concentrating its *content* on the outer world, and by using *methods* that prevent us from learning how to flow back and forth between the inner and the outer. It amounts to what Reg Revans has called 'the idolization of past experience' – from which stem all sorts of limitations on creativity and learning.

One of these limitations is that, as a result, we are encouraged to have touching faith in, and emotional dependency upon, 'experts', who usually act as a convenient armour against the necessity to think for oneself. They also provide us with a perfect scapegoat when things go wrong. (This is made worse by the fact that many experts only serve the ends of their political or commercial patrons. It's always amazing how 'independent experts' appointed by, say, the dairy industry, or the electricity board, come up with very different opinions from those retained by the margarine industry, or the ecology movement.)

Instead we need, in this late industrial era, to become empowered to act and to learn from action. We must develop sufficient confidence and ability to think for ourselves. Certainly we may seek *information* (but very rarely advice) from others; but – acting together with our colleagues and others involved (see Chapter 2) – we have to come to our own decisions, be responsible for our own actions. Paulo Freire said that education is either for liberation or for domination; self-management is about learning for liberation – liberating ourselves and our organizations from their chronic 'stuckness'.

So another key element of self-management is self-empowering – and with it, of course, that extra degree of responsibility that comes with power; the responsibility to recognize it, tap it, use it positively and beneficially. No one is suggesting that awareness and self-management necessarily lead to a more comfortable life. Indeed, sometimes the opposite is true.

Another characteristic of the old form of thinking about managing is that it encourages us to rely upon role models from the past. Thus, Colonel Urwick brought his chains of command and spans of control from the army into industry; most books on managing are based upon the 'manufacturing model' of organization, including the recent endorsement of virile oriental practices, ignoring the fact that these days this has become a minor sector of employment in so-called developed economies. Again, virtually all books on managing are written by men and yet the labour force has always included large numbers of women.

This is not to belittle the wisdom of the past, but to look at it in its proper perspective as 'this is what worked – or not, as the case may be – last time, for other people'. We are *not* advocating a new regime of mere navel-gazing; we are *not* decrying theory; we are *not* pressing for action at the expense of understanding. But we do want to strengthen a new tradition that is finding increasing favour. This tends to be known as a self-management or self- development approach. What are its main features?

In terms of the ideas that we have been looking at in this chapter, this new, synergistic approach takes a 'both —— and ——' view of managing and developing. Thus, it focuses

- both on the inner and the outer, recognizing that in general these are inextricably linked, and that neither can really be understood in isolation from the other
- on managing both myself and my environment, again in the realization that

I cannot understand or manage others until I can understand
or manage myself
and that conversely
I cannot understand or manage myself until I can understand
and manage others
- on being responsible to and for both myself and my environment, that is,
    I need to understand and take into account both my own
    needs and those of others
    and
    I need to understand and be aware of the consequences of my
    actions both for myself and for others
- both on theory and on practice, by
    using my real-life questions, issues and problems as the basic
    starting point in my need and search for established
    knowledge
    and by
    using my real-life experiences as an opportunity to derive and
    generate my own meanings and understandings

This is the approach that we are trying to bring into our work, both
with individuals and with organizations. It is also the approach that
we want to take in this book – to work with you, the reader, in
managing yourself along the lines just given. Indeed, we might say
that this is the purpose of the book.

So how can we make a start on this? What is inside that inner
circle in Figure 1.1 – the part that represents 'managing ME'?

SURVIVAL, MAINTENANCE AND DEVELOPMENT

To start with, let's look at another idea about what is involved in
the process of 'managing ME'. This is that in our lives at home, or
at work, or elsewhere, we can be described as being engaged at
any given time in *surviving, developing* or *maintaining*. What do
we mean by this?

Surviving means keeping going when things seem pretty awful; not going under, keeping your head above water, avoiding collapse, disaster or destruction. Although it can therefore be seen as a minimal level of functioning, rather than a desirable one, it is nonetheless something that we all experience, that each of us, at times, recognizes as the best that we can do, the most we can hope for.

SURVIVING

At this point it might be useful to examine some of your own survival experiences. (You can do this in your head or, better still, jot them down on a piece of paper or, as already suggested, in a special self-management notebook or diary.) Try to recall three or four occasions in your life when you were fighting hard to survive. Then, for each example, note how it felt at the time; what in fact kept you going. And, once that period was over, what was its effect on you? Were you in any way different? How did it affect other people around you, at work and/or at home?

One of the things that you may well find emerges from this little exercise is the importance of support while working at survival. Some people seek the support of tranquillizers; these may provide an essential immediate-term crutch, but they don't really have anything positive to offer in the long run. (The same is even more true of that other form of 'instant support', namely alcohol.) Far better – although perhaps harder to come by – is the support of other people, either individually or in groups. (See especially Chapter 7.) Not only can this support 'keep you going through the night', but it can help you gradually to make sense out of what is happening, so that you can begin moving into the 'developing' mode.

Let's look next, then, at *development*. As before, we suggest that you think about three or four occasions in your life when, you think, you developed. What were these occasions? How did you feel at the time? What were the effects on you, and on others around you?

Some of these developmental events may be the same survival episodes that you have already considered – although obviously there probably won't be an exact overlap; just as not all crises lead to development, neither is all development brought about by crisis. Nonetheless, there often *is* a link between the two; development often comes from crisis, and crisis often leads to development. Why should this be?

To answer this we need first to look at what we mean by development. Although the term is often used fairly loosely, in this book we are taking it to refer to a qualitative change in the way you are. Some dictionary definitions include

- bringing out what is latent or potential in
- bringing to a more advanced state
- working out the potentialities of
- causing to grow or advance
- advancing through successive stages to a more fully grown state
- opening out

So what does this mean for development as a manager?

Well, it might be a new skill; a new way of seeing things; a new attitude; or a new set of feelings; a new level of consciousness, or mode of managing (see Chapter 3). The important word in all of these is *new*. Development is not just more of something that you have already; it is not just an increase of knowledge, or a higher degree of an existing skill. Development is a *different* state of being or functioning, rather than a mere topping up of something that you already have.

Are all qualitative changes developmental? Presumably not – the change has somehow to be experienced as 'good', or 'bene-

23

ficial', or 'in the right direction'. Thus, if you look at your own list of events, and the effects they had on you, you will almost certainly have chosen some that you think were in some way or other positive. Of course, only you can judge whether or not a particular outcome was good or bad news, and that judgement will depend on all sorts of things, related to you, your job, your home, the way you are, your personality, what's happening in your life, and so on.

We can now examine why it is that development is so often linked with crisis, which is very often the initiating cause of development. It is when things start to go wrong, when we get a surprise or a shock, that we come face to face with the realization that our existing views on the world, on work, on relationships etc. are no longer as valid as we thought previously. Let's take another short case example.

Musa Mohammed had carefully and successfully climbed the tree of promotion in an engineering company, and was now, at forty-two, an assistant chief design engineer. He confidently expected to succeed his boss who was retiring in two months' time. It therefore came as a severe shock when he was told that it had been decided to appoint someone from outside, in order to bring some new ideas into the company.

So Musa's view – of the company, his job, himself – has suddenly been invalidated. How can he respond to this? Obviously, one way will be to become very bitter, angry ('bunch of racist bastards') and so on. Indeed, disbelief followed by anger are the usual reactions to shock or crisis; the important thing is to be aware of this and then to move on, rather than remaining negative for the rest of your life.

This is where support is so vital. Let us suppose that Musa is lucky in this respect. He has a good friend who is not only supportive in the traditional sense, but who also cares enough for him to take the risk of giving Musa some feedback. So after an initial period of listening sympathetically, he suggests that his friend perhaps has been a bit stick-in-the-mud, that he has in fact at times refused to consider new ideas, pooh-poohed latest thinking, and so on.

At first Musa can't believe his ears. Here is his old friend more or less saying it's all his own fault! However, deep down inside he is able to recognize that there is a lot of truth in this. Gradually, again with support from friends, family and his new boss, he changes his image of himself, realizing that he has to develop a new attitude towards innovation. He then goes on to start finding out much more about latest thinking, which he begins to find really interesting. After three years his whole approach to the job has changed, and he is also much more likely to get a more senior post, either within his present company or elsewhere.

Here, then, the shock or crisis is the first, precipitating step towards development. Initial feelings of disbelief, anger, dismay, pain, grief etc. *can* be transformed into the starting point for development, especially if we have a network of support to keep us going. The alternative, leading to a more or less permanent slide into continuing anger, depression, demotivation or even self-destruction – is all too easy. We will look at this again in Chapter 3.

Another link between shock and development arises from the fact that, in acquiring a new perspective on the world, we are letting go of a part of our former selves and this is very likely to be stressful, since we are in effect saying goodbye to something that has been important to us. Even when we can clearly see that the change is for the better, it is often hard to let go of a cherished idea, value, ambition, relationship, person, job, place or whatever. Often, at this stage, we are beset with doubt, or guilt, or feelings of not having made the best use of time or opportunities in the past. For example,

Tom's eldest daughter Alison recently left home, at eighteen, to go and work in Paris. She left on good terms, no feelings of rancour or rejection, and the whole thing was in fact a very natural development: she became independent, he became the

25

father of an independent woman, as opposed to a dependent girl. Nonetheless, for some days he was filled with feelings of regret, and doubt as to whether he could have been 'a better father', mooning over family photographs, and so on.

So even developments that come our way more or less naturally, and that can be seen as basically 'good' right from the start, are often experienced as shocks, crises etc.

We can now look at where *maintenance* comes in. The most obvious example is with physical maintenance – keeping fit. If you are physically fit, then a shock is much less likely to give you a heart attack.

But what about more general fitness? Indeed, what does the word 'fit' mean? The *Chambers Dictionary* gives as its main definition 'in suitable condition' and 'well trained and ready'. So maintenance can be seen as getting ready for development – keeping up to date, watching what's going on, keeping in good physical condition, building and maintaining a support network, and acquiring certain skills (such as observation, reflection, self-awareness) that are needed if you are to transform crisis into development.

So maintenance is more than surviving, but compared with developing it is fairly static, and there is a danger that you can become complacent, content with mere maintenance, avoiding the challenge of change and development. The question for the 'keep-fit freak' should be, 'What am I getting ready for?'

These three main processes involved in 'managing ME' are shown diagrammatically in Figure 1.4. Placing maintenance between surviving and developing shows its other value, as a period of recuperation from the excitement and exhaustion of the other two. The arrows are intended to show that all three are linked in a continuous flow, and that each is equally important. So once again this is a case of 'both —— and ——' rather than 'either —— or ——'. Survival is essential, but to get anywhere you must sooner or later move into a development phase; getting ready, keeping fit, is very useful provided you realize you are getting ready to do something; developing is fine, but if you don't spare time for maintenance or consolidation you will wear yourself out with frenzied changes.

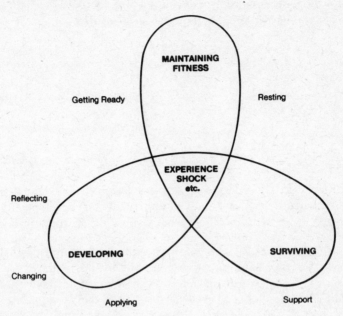

Figure 1.4

MANAGING EFFECTIVELY

Let us now turn to another key notion of self-management. This is the idea that, broadly speaking, there are four aspects of ourselves in which we need to survive, maintain and develop. These are:

- *health*: a sound mind in a sound body
- *skills*: mental, technical, social, artistic
- *action*: getting things done in the world
- *identity*: knowing who you are, accepting yourself while having an idea of who you want to become

Of course, there is a link between these four; you need health if you are to become skilful, or to get things done. Similarly, getting something done requires skill, as well as motivation. And your skill is bound up with the way you see and value yourself. So we can show them all as being linked as in Figure 1.5.

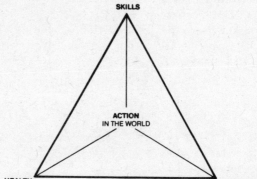

Figure 1.5

Although in a way it's a bit arbitrary (since each is linked with the three others), we have put *action* in the middle since, in the end, as a manager it's what you do that matters. There's no point having good health, skills and self-identity if you don't apply these to some useful end; indeed, you could say that this is a criminal or moral waste of talent. So for the New Age manager, the bottom line is what we do, as a result of taking responsibility for ourselves. We can illustrate the interplay of these factors from the experience of a manager:

A few months ago Marion applied for promotion. Unfortunately, she came up against an extremely sexist senior manager at the interview, who challenged her most aggressively and told her that as far as he was concerned she wasn't to be trusted, as she was quite likely to become pregnant and demand a lot of time off. Marion became flustered at this, and the rest of the interview went badly. As a result of this experience, she has labelled herself as 'no good at interviews' – i.e. part of her self-image is that of someone who is – and therefore always will be – unable to handle an interview properly.

Now her boss has put her forward again to be reconsidered. She has many of the qualifications and qualities required for the new job, but she still has her negative self-image as far as interviews are concerned. Consequently, she feels uncertain and unconfident. Because of this, she is very nervous. She wants to do well but when the time comes she doesn't have the willpower to overcome this and in fact gets tongue-tied; she isn't able to do herself justice, to show what she is indeed capable of.

Here is an all too familiar case of lack of skill (in handling unfair confrontation or criticism – see Chapter 3) leading to a negative view of the self, which in turn reduces skill even further, in a vicious circle. This area of working on your sense of identity, your self-image, is vital if you are to manage yourself effectively, and we will devote Chapters 3 and 4 to it.

Now, though, let's look back again at Marion's experience – in particular, at her second interview. The main points can be abstracted as follows:

- She has labelled herself as 'no good at interviews'. That is, she *thinks* of herself as a bad interviewee.
- She *feels* uncertain and unconfident.
- She doesn't have the *willpower* to overcome this . . . isn't able to do herself justice.

Here we have, in italic print, three basic inner processes that very much affect our behaviour – namely:

- Thinking: your ideas, thoughts, perceptions, concepts, theories, beliefs, values.
- Feeling: your emotions, moods, feelings.
- Willing or doing: your intentions, motives, drives.

These three play a large part in determining our behaviour. In Marion's case, her negative thoughts about herself contributed to her feeling unconfident, and these two reinforced each other so that her intention or desire to do well was overpowered. Consequently, she was unable to manage herself in the way that she would have liked.

In order to manage yourself, then, you need to be able to manage your thinking, your feeling, and your willing. We will be stressing this point many times throughout this book.

So far we have seen that there are four aspects of the self that need managing (health, skills, action and identity), together with three inner processes (thinking, feeling and willing). We can now bring these together as summarized in Table 1.1, which is derived from recent research[1] about the characteristics of effective managers.

This table shows some of the characteristics or attributes that are required if you are to be successful at managing either yourself or others. You can see that in a way it might be said to be reflected in the basic structure of this book, as it also shows the chapters that concentrate on various sets of attributes.

HELPING OTHERS MANAGE

For a moment, though, let's stop thinking about managing ME and think of all the others with whom we work and live. Perhaps we have made the case for managing ME as far as you the reader are concerned. If you could get your goals and priorities sorted out, get to work on surviving, maintaining and developing the thinking, feeling and willing aspects of your health, skills, action and identity, then obviously you'll be making progress!

We all live and work with others – no one is an island, and so on – and their lives and concerns are a part of us, just as ours are a part of them. In thinking about managing, more than with most other activities, we need to consider how managing ME in a different way is going to affect these important others.

The most obvious criticism of managing ME is that it is selfish.

[1] M. Leary *et al.*, *The Stages of Managerial Development*, Manpower Services Commission, Sheffield, 1985.

Table 1.1

Aspects of the self that require managing	Inner processes that require managing			
	Thinking	Feeling	Willing or doing	
Health: a sound mind in a sound body	Holistic thinking, which includes avoidance of simplistic stereotyping and compartmentalizing; recognition of the way in which things are interrelated and interdependent; thinking in terms of 'both . . . and . . .'. Ability to remain open-minded, to suspend judgement.	Awareness and acknowledgement of feelings (you have feelings, rather than feelings having you). Balance, inner calm.	Physical exercise, diet, nutrition. Healthy habits and lifestyle.	See Chapter 6.
Skills	Mental and conceptual skills; e.g., memory, logic, creativity, intuition.	Interpersonal, social, expressive and artistic skills.	Physical, mechanical and technical skills.	See Chapter 5.
Action in the world: getting things done	Ability to make your own decisions, for yourself, as well as being open to suggestions and feedback from others. Decisions made with an understanding of the way in which your actions affect other people, and have consequences for them as well as for you.	Concern both for your own interests and for those of other people – thus, making moral decisions.	Going out and taking initiatives; courage. Managing and transforming setbacks, disappointments, frustration; determination.	See Chapter 2.
Identity, self	Personal values, ethical and moral standards, and philosophical, spiritual and/or religious beliefs. Awareness and understanding of these and of other aspects of self. Knowing yourself.	Recognizing your strengths and rejoicing in them; accepting yourself in spite of your weaknesses. Valuing yourself.	Self-motivation, purpose in life; sense of security, faith and hope. Being yourself.	See Chapters 3 and 4.

Managing Yourself

Surely managing is first and foremost about working with and through other people. Focusing on oneself is self-indulgent, even narcissistic.

Well, it is true that a self-managing or self-developing approach is selfish. You do start from your own needs, your strengths, your weaknesses, your goals, and so on. This is where we come up against two opposing traditions, one of selfless denial, the other of selfish domination. Both of these can be seen to be undesirable; we need a positive synthesis of the two.

Let's start with the honourable tradition in managing which holds that managers should do the job in a selfless way, seeing themselves not only in charge of, but also responsible for, those they work with. We don't want to lose all the elements of this tradition – after all, we would probably not think much of the captain who was first into the lifeboats! However, if this belief takes you to the point of not thinking about yourself enough to keep up to date, to learn new skills, or if you don't look after yourself and take insufficient time out with your family, then as a manager you are not only failing yourself, but you are setting a very bad example for others.

The trouble is that when you start to take on a 'managing ME first' approach it might often seem to fall into the other tradition – that of naked self-interest before anything else, no matter what the cost to others. Thus, it might seem selfish to people who are used to seeing you behave in more selfless ways; perhaps more importantly, it may seem selfish and 'wrong' to you yourself, who are saying, in effect, 'Now it's my turn.' To say, for example, 'From now on I'm going to take half a day a week out to read and to think', or to say, 'You and the children can look after yourselves a bit more because I'm going out to work' requires courage.

But it need not be selfish if – unlike those currently operating in the me-first-no-matter-what-the-cost fashion so prevalent in many managers – we can *balance* our own needs with those of others. (In particular, those who are important to us, but ideally more or less everybody else who is affected by what we do.)

We inherit from our parents and our early upbringing many

useful ideas and rules about behaving responsibly and thinking of others. We have to learn early on not just to think of ourselves, but to recognize that others have rights too. We have to learn to share our toys and take our turn.

Later in life, as mothers, fathers, husbands, wives, managers, neighbours, we get a lot of practice at putting the needs of others first, and there is a good chance of getting out of balance – of forgetting about our own needs, or thinking that these needs, although felt, are not really legitimate.

The big problem about behaving selflessly all the time is that you get stuck. You get stuck with all the jobs no one else wants; you stick yourself with all the jobs you've always done for fear of upsetting people; but worst of all you're stuck because you can't change, move or develop. This is simply because changing or developing means that you have to think about YOU – your needs, goals, abilities, constraints, opportunities, situation, day-dreams, fears, ambitions, responsibilities, feelings, loves, hates. . . . How can you think about these if you are selfless all the time?

Stuckness is one of the most serious problems that sap the vitality of our organizations too. It's not as easy to recognize as foreign competition, exchange rates or strikes, and therefore it remains largely hidden from sight until special circumstances bring out some equivalent of the 'Dunkirk spirit' and we all amaze ourselves with how much we can achieve. The main cause of ineffectiveness in organizations – and the larger they are, the more this is true – is the number of people in them who are stuck. These people are stuck perhaps in limited jobs, or stuck at limited levels of knowledge, skill or vision in doing their jobs; or stuck with no ambition or desire to do better any more. We call them variously bureaucrats, sleepers, demotivated, fed up, bored or lazy, timeservers, clockwatchers, skivers and a host of other names.

Whatever has caused it for each person, they have switched off or limited their effort as far as this organization at least is concerned, and perhaps in the rest of their lives. Stuckness is not simply a problem of ageing – we all know twenty-five-year-olds

33

who are stuck and sixty-five-year-olds who are not but who are still puzzling, enquiring and changing their minds. It is perilously easy to get stuck. All you have to do is to stop managing yourself.

Sometimes, of course, this stuckness comes to a violent head. We can hold our needs down, perhaps not even being conscious of them ourselves, until one day . . . whoosh!!! . . . an explosion, with lots of energy, excitement, but also casualties. For suddenly discovering these needs after years of repression can make us very angry, and in our anger we may not know our strength, hurting and blaming those people unfortunate enough to be within reach.

As adults it is a vital part of our own development to review those childhood messages and principles that we have come to live by, and see how relevant they are to our current life situation. Is such-and-such behaviour a compulsion, an empty ritual, a way of avoiding upsetting someone whose anger I fear, or on whose favour or patronage I depend? Or is it indeed a useful, satisfying rule of conduct? For one of the key aspects of a healthy style of self-management is that I decide for myself what rules, customs etc. are productive and appropriate, and then try to live by these, whether or not they fit current norms and expectations.

Managing yourself as an adult requires that you make a conscious decision to learn and develop by looking at past experiences in the context of your current needs, and deciding whether to stick or to try to change. We owe it to ourselves and to the others around us *not* to deny and repress our needs, but to become more aware of them and to consider how they can be met, *along with* the needs of others. In so doing – in breaking away from 'either my needs or yours' to 'let's try to meet both mine and yours' – you may be saving more than just your own life.

So managing ME is not just a selfish pursuit, but a necessary step for us in our organizations if we – us and our organizations – are to remain alive and healthy. Here, a middle manager in a large public service organization describes the problem as she sees it and as it affects her:

How much can we continue to change? You see people hanging

on, hanging on even at forty-eight or forty-nine to pension rights, security and so on. I think a lot of stress in middle management is caused by this. People go to ground, entrench and hide themselves, half-knowing they are not performing well, but hiding the evidence. I'm being told to rattle the sabre around them, but I think this will only make them worse. They're often nice people, gentle, kind and simple, you can't call them in and tell them their work is no good. They need help, they're often doing their best in their own way and we don't have the resources to help.

It has started me thinking about my own career. I'm only thirty-eight and I don't want to end up like this. Why is it that with some people the years just become increasingly painful for themselves and for those around them, while others provide good models right into their sixties . . . of changing themselves and helping people around them to change?

So, NOT getting stuck involves managing ME, surviving, maintaining myself and developing myself. This is not purely selfish because the renewal of other people – in organizations, communities, even societies – depends, at root, on the efforts of individuals. Like its antidote – enthusiasm – stuckness is contagious. It infects us and we infect others. When we get set in our ways, feel that 'we have arrived' or otherwise limit ourselves, we are contributing to the stuckness of others and of organizations.

2 Getting things done

In the Introduction we looked at the process of managing a situation – and yourself – in terms of warming up to it, shedding light on it, weighing it up and then doing something. Then, in Chapter 1, we noticed (Figure 1.5) that managing yourself involves four dimensions – your identity, skills, health and action in the world, with *action* in the centre of the triangle, since managing is about doing.

So we are now going to focus on the planning and carrying out of action – i.e. we are looking at *action* first from Table 1.1. For convenience, that section of the table is reproduced here, as Table 2.1.

Table 2.1

Aspects of the self that require managing	*Inner processes* that require managing		
	Thinking	*Feeling*	*Willing* or *doing*
Action in the world: getting things done	Ability to make your own decisions, for yourself, as well as being open to suggestions and feedback from others. Decisions made with an understanding of the way in which your actions affect other people, and have consequences for them as well as for you.	Concern both for your own interests and for those of other people – thus, making moral decisions.	Going out and taking initiatives; courage. Managing and transforming setbacks, disappointments, frustration; determination.

You will find lots of ideas about warming up and shedding light – i.e. on analysis and understanding – in subsequent chapters. What we want to do here is to look at how you can move from understanding into planning and then doing. Hence, we will be looking at the following:

Weighing up
1 Prioritizing and clarifying your aims or *intentions*
2 Generating alternative courses of action
3 Evaluating the alternative courses of action
4 Deciding which course of action to take – i.e. making your *resolutions*

Taking action
5 Planning what you are going to do – your *first steps*
6 Carrying out first step – *action*
7 Reviewing and planning *next step* and so on

Before that, though, you might find it helpful to think about yourself and the way you set about action now. Use the following questions as a way into this; you can either think about them to yourself, or go through them with a speaking partner. But don't be in too much of a hurry; you may find it better to mull over some of them for a day or two; or come back to them from time to time. Don't necessarily try to answer them all at one sitting.

QUESTIONNAIRE ABOUT THE WAY YOU TAKE ACTION IN THE WORLD

1 How do you decide on priorities, choose between competing aims and goals? What factors do you take into account? On reflection, can you think of other factors that you ignore, but that might usefully be taken into account? Can you illustrate with examples?

2 When making a decision, how do you generate alternative

courses of action? How do you decide or choose between these alternatives? Again, what factors do you take into account? And what of other possible factors?

3 What have been the two or three most difficult decisions you have had to make in the past twelve months or so? Why were these difficult? What and who were involved? How did you go about it? What do you now think about the way you handled it, and about what happened? What are your feelings about it?

4 Can you see any patterns in the way you respond to particular types of decision-making situations?

5 How do you feel when you encounter setbacks, when what you are trying to do doesn't seem to be going too well, when the going gets tough? What effects do these feelings have?

6 Looking at your answers to these questions, do you think others would agree that that's how you are? That is, do they see you in the same way as you see yourself? Are you sure? How can you find out?

7 What are your thoughts as a result of looking at – or better still, attempting to answer – these questions? How are your feelings? Do you want to do anything as a result? If not, why not? And if so, what are you actually going to do?

PRIORITIZING; CLARIFYING YOUR INTENTIONS

In your life as a manager – or indeed simply (?!) as a human being – you are faced with many issues and questions, about which you have to take decisions, make plans, take actions. Sometimes it's very clear where to start – although even then it might very well be worth stopping a minute and asking yourself if you are quite sure. Is the priority as clear-cut as you are making out? Would others agree with you? What assumptions are you making here?

At times, though, it's useful to take a slightly more systematic approach to priority setting. The first step in this process is to identify the questions coming your way.

Questions coming your way

By 'questions coming your way' we mean those issues that you have to tackle if you are to survive, develop or get ready and fit (see Chapter 1). That is, something you have to accomplish if you are to manage yourself effectively. In anyone's life, there are many such questions and issues. Some are bombarding us all too clearly (although in such cases the *real* question might actually be rather well disguised). Others are there if we only recognize them; and others still are almost over the horizon – giving us the choice of proactively seeking them out or waiting, more reactively, until they hit us.

Perhaps it would be useful here to give some examples of the sort of things we are talking about. (You will find ways of exploring most of these in detail in subsequent chapters.)

- Issues connected with my work; something to do with what's expected of me in my job, or in my role, that requires better self-management, such as taking a risk; confronting a problem rather than avoiding it.
- Questions coming from other people; things that others are saying to me, or asking me; relationships that need changing one way or another; unfinished business with somebody.
- Questions arising from my life – past and future; throwing off burdens or hindrances from the past; recognizing positive things and seeing where they might lead; looking for opportunities, challenges, purpose in the future; coming to terms with getting older, and seeing what this means both in the way of limitations and of opportunities.
- Issues to do with me, my personality, the way I am; my health, skills, sense of identity; my style and/or mode of managing; my stage of development.

Just reading this list may start to give you an idea of some of the issues that you need to be facing up to. If so, that's fine. However, the *main* purpose of this chapter is to examine ways of moving from an understanding of the issues into deciding what to do about them (intentions) and then planning action (resolutions) and carrying these out. This will equip you to move into the action phase when, in subsequent chapters, we look at ways of developing your awareness of what issues you should usefully be working on.

How you read this chapter will depend on how you are approaching it. You may *now* be aware of some question(s)/ issue(s) facing you. If so, you can immediately try out the action-process that we are about to describe.

On the other hand, you may not at this time be at all sure what your questions are. In that case, you can either skip this chapter and come back to it after some of the others or, preferably, read through it now so as to get some idea of the action-process, as that may help you to see the practical implications of the subsequent chapters when you come to them.

Getting an overview of your questions and issues

Assuming, then, that you are aware of a number of questions and issues facing you, how do you set about getting these into some sort of priority? It's useful here to try to get an overall picture, using a technique such as Domain Mapping.

DOMAIN MAPPING

This technique can be used right through the action-process, so we will be referring to it several times in this chapter. Do you remember Peter, the personnel manager in Chapter 1? As an example we will be working with his map, which is shown in Figure 2.1.

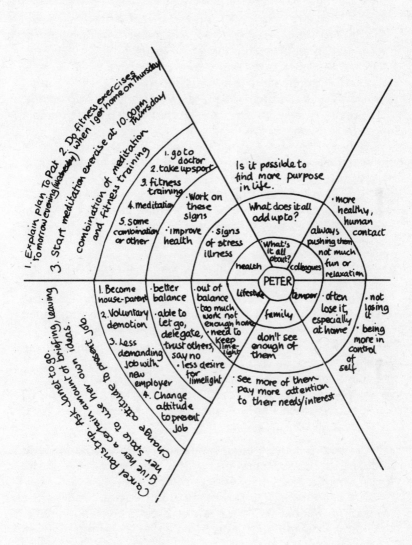

Figure 2.1 Peter's domain map

As you will see, the domain map consists of a series of rings, like a dart board, with you at the centre – the bull's eye. The 'board' is divided up into a number of segments, or 'domains', one for each question or issue.

In the first ring away from the bull, you write in, in each segment, the question you are working on. This is done by considering that you are in some sort of relationship with it; i.e. a relationship with a person; a task; some part of yourself/ your personality; or whatever.

Then, in the next ring, you write in a brief description of how things are with that relationship/aspect of your life at present.

Thus, Peter has identified five areas or 'relationships' that are causing him concern – that require action if he is to manage himself more effectively. As you can see from the figure, these are:

- with his colleagues – Peter is always pushing them; no chance for fun or relaxation with them
- with his temper – Peter loses it often, especially at home ('the children seem to be growing up fast without much help from him and since Pat returned to work . . .')
- with his lifestyle – he's always rushing about all over the place
- with his health ('headache . . . bloody rheumatism')
- with a nagging doubt, only half-formed (or half-allowed?) about whether what he does is all that important ('What does it all add up to?')

The next step is to go out another ring and write in how you would like that aspect/relationship to be. You can see in the diagram what Peter has written in for each.

We will come back to the remaining three rings later. In the meantime, the picture so far can be used to give an overview of your issues and questions, as an aid to choosing priorities and clarifying *intentions*.

Clarifying intentions

By *intention* we mean here the choice of issue to work on, and the desired end result. In terms of the figure, this is represented by the third ring away from the bull, in the segment(s) chosen as priority.

So, how do you choose this priority area? This will of course very much depend on you. However, we can easily identify some of the criteria that you can use when making your decision – although the choice is yours.

You might decide that the priority area is one which, as far as you can judge:

- is the most important; in some way it matters most, it's the one you really want or need to tackle; it will have the biggest pay-off – for yourself and/or for others
- will have the quickest pay-off – i.e. will show some results very soon (if you are lucky there may be one with both the biggest and quickest pay-off; often, though, there will have to be some trade-off between speed and effect)
- can be said to be the most urgent – i.e. the effects of *not* tackling it will be the most disastrous and/or will be felt soonest
- will be the easiest to tackle ('let's start gradually where some good results are most likely')
- will be the most difficult to tackle ('let's start with the big one; if I can handle that I'll be able to handle anything')
- can be seen as a 'key' one – that is, in some way connected with many of the others, so that working on this one will also lead to progress on the others; or, unless and until this one is resolved, nothing can be done about the others

Coming back to our case study, after thinking about it Peter decides that his priority area is working on his lifestyle, since this is playing a significant part in causing some of his other difficulties, such as signs of stress disease, not seeing enough of his family, losing his temper and, to some extent, the unsatisfactory relationships with his colleagues.

43

He realizes, though, that it will be some time before the effects of this will be fully felt, and he wants to make an immediate start on improving his health. So these two are his immediate *intentions*.

ALTERNATIVE COURSES OF ACTION

'There are more ways than one of skinning a cat.' At the risk of offending cat lovers, this phrase indicates that there are usually a number of alternative routes to a given goal. A lot depends, obviously, on what that goal is. In some cases, there are a number of fairly simple, clear-cut actions that can be readily identified, while other goals may be such that appropriate steps are not as easy to recognize.

Let's return to Peter. His short-term intention of improving his health, particularly by working on his stress-related symptoms, is relatively straightforward. For example, he could:

1 Go to the doctor and get drugs (painkillers, tranquillizers).
2 Take up a sport – e.g. squash, which a lot of his colleagues play.
3 Start a programme of physical fitness training.
4 Start a programme of meditation.
5 Some combination of the above.

It's not always as easy or as clear as this, of course. So with Peter's longer-term intention – to change his lifestyle – there are no relatively simple techniques or exercises that he can carry out.

When working on bigger issues like this, it can be useful to think in terms of there being four broad strategies from which you can constructively choose.

1 *Change the situation*: confront Anne, with whom you are having a difficult time; demand that the marketing department gives you more notice of special promotion offers coming along so as to give your production department more chance to handle the extra output; make improvements to the recruitment system; explain to Richard how he can do his job properly, so that you are not lumbered with picking up his mistakes.

2 *Change yourself*: perhaps Anne has a point – you are being unreasonable; perhaps you should be more available and open when the marketing manager does try to come and discuss things with you; perhaps you want Richard to make mistakes, so that you can show how clever you are. So you may need to examine and change your own behaviour, your attitude, take a different perspective, listen to others, acquire new skill or knowledge.

3 *Leave the situation*: find as constructive and generally positive a way as possible of moving on – that is, constructive to you and, ideally, constructive for the others involved. At very least, try to minimize the destructive effects of your moving. Check to make sure you are not jumping from the frying pan into the fire. And look out for signs that you are actually trying to make things as difficult as possible for others when you leave – 'I'll show those bastards, I'll take all the forecasting data with me, so they'll have to go over it all again!'; 'I'll teach that bloody trainer a lesson, putting me in a position where I've had to quit the course – I'll write to his boss with some story of gross incompetence and professional malpractice!'

4 *Decide to live with the situation*, but come to terms with it. Shrug your shoulders; say, 'You can't win them all'; make Elisabeth a less important part of your life – it's more her loss than yours; give in graciously; or keep at it and give yourself rewards and treats for sticking with it. The important thing about deciding to live with it is that you *don't* continue to moan, groan or fret about it, and you don't allow it to give you negative feelings about yourself or the other people involved. You move on, psychologically if not physically.

This is where working with a partner, or in a group (as discussed in Chapter 7) can be so useful, either as a source of *information* (which, as we stress in that chapter, is very different from advice, which in general is to be avoided!), or to act as a sounding-board for you to think aloud with, bounce ideas off, get feedback and so on.

The way Peter' life is, it's not likely that he will immediately think of finding such a speaking partner. So for the time being at any rate he'll have to rely on his own ideas. Or . . . wait! Another of his areas of concern was his relationship with his family. Could he not talk through his intention with his wife, Pat?

This raises a difficult question. For it is often very difficult to explore issues objectively with other people who are closely involved in, and affected by, them. The very fact that they are so involved makes it almost impossible for them to remain detached, to look objectively at all the pros and cons. This is why, of course, it is often helpful for parties in a conflict to seek assistance from an uninvolved third party, such as an arbitrator, or a marriage guidance counsellor. Because, ideally, if you are to be helpful when listening and counselling somebody, you need to be able to enter that discussion in a free state – i.e. in such a state that you are in no way looking for, wanting, hoping for, expecting, desiring or in any way seeking/wishing to gain anything from that person.

So, knowing this either consciously or subconsciously, Peter decides not to talk about this with Pat – not for the time being, anyway.

After much thought, then, he is able to generate alternative strategies:

1 Give up his job, become a house-parent and depend financially on Pat's earnings.
2 Remain with the bank, but ask to be transferred to a less demanding job (i.e. seek voluntary demotion).
3 Seek a less demanding job with another employer.
4 Remain in the same job, but change his attitude, approach and style to it – e.g. delegate more, trust others more, learn to say 'No' more often, lessen his desire always to be in the forefront, in the limelight.

In fact, looking at that fourth one, it appears that it might actually contain within it a whole new issue for Peter – a new segment in his domain map – namely 'his desire always to be in the forefront, in the limelight'. This illustrates that this whole action-process, although described for convenience in seven discrete steps, is in reality an iterative process; that is, it often involves a rather messy-looking to-ing and fro-ing, going back to an earlier step and modifying it, then forward a bit, back again, forward but in a different direction, and so on. 'Three steps forward, two steps backwards and one step sideways,' as Malcolm Leary once put it.

However, in this case we'll continue to subsume all that under the one domain of Peter's lifestyle.

EVALUATING THE ALTERNATIVE COURSES OF ACTION; COMING TO YOUR RESOLUTION

Evaluating the alternatives entails weighing up the pros and cons, advantages and disadvantages, of each. These can be considered in two groups – pros/cons in terms of practicability; and pros/cons in terms of likely effects.

Practicability involves thinking about the degree to which the possible action is realistic. So we need to consider things like the resources required and available, possible obstructions or resistance, as well as positive factors that will help.

Separate from this is the question of the effects of the action. To what extent is it likely to achieve your goal? What possible side-effects (negative or positive) might there be? What will be the consequences for other people, as well as for yourself?

A useful way of looking at these various questions is through a technique known as force-field analysis.

Force-field analysis

Although this sounds rather complex and sophisticated, it is in fact very simple, and is a useful way of getting an overall picture of the helping and hindering factors related to a proposed course of action. We will return to the case study of Peter to illustrate it.

Let's look at one of his alternative ways of moving towards his intention of improving his health. It doesn't matter which one we take – it would be sensible to do a force-field analysis on each of his possible five solutions. We haven't got the space here to do that, so we might as well look at the first – namely '*Go to the doctor for painkillers and tranquillizers*'.

Figure 2.2 shows the start of the force-field analysis. You will see that this simply involves drawing a line, representing where you are now, with a big arrow upwards in the direction of where you want to be – i.e. aiming at your intention.

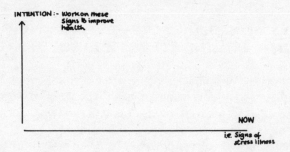

Figure 2.2

You then take the course of action that you are considering (i.e. in this case, 'going to the doctor . . .') and think of all the good and bad things related to it, its pros/cons, etc. You draw these in on the diagram, representing them as an arrow either pointing upwards if that factor is in the action's favour (i.e. will help you be successful in succeeding in your intention) or downwards for hindering, unhelpful factors and disadvantages. You will also notice that the arrows vary in length; the idea is to give some approximation of quantification, of your judgement or opinion of the *strength* of a particular force, and making the arrow-length proportional to this.

Thus, in Figure 2.3 Peter considers that the fact that going to the doctor will not help him with his other intention of changing his lifestyle is more important/significant than the fact that it is easy; and the fact that it is easy is less significant than its probably short-term effectiveness – which is much less important, thinks Peter, than its probable long-term ineffectiveness.

48

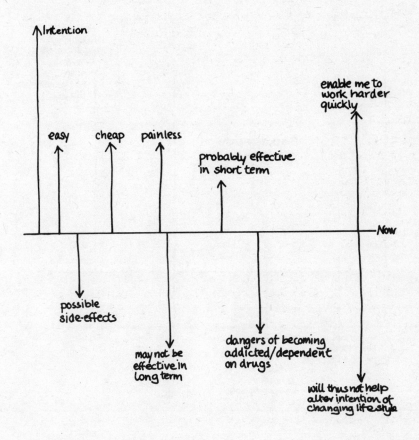

Figure 2.3 Alternative no. 1: Go to doctor for painkillers and tranquillizers

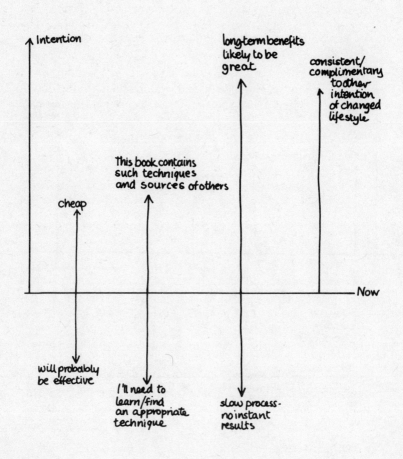

Intention

long-term benefits
likely to be
great

consistent/
complimentary
to other
intention
of changed
lifestyle

This book contains
such techniques
and sources of others

cheap

Now

will probably
be effective

I'll need to
learn/find
an appropriate
technique

slow process-
no instant
results

Figure 2.4 Alternative no. 4: Meditation

As we have said, you need to do this type of analysis for each of the possible actions; we show just one more here, that for '*meditation*' (Figure 2.4). It's clear from comparing the figures that of these two, anyway, 'meditation' is the better bet. In fact, doing an analysis for all of them led Peter to his *resolution*: a combination of meditation and fitness; he abandoned the idea of squash because it was relatively expensive, would take him out of the house even more, and, he decided, would add to his feelings of competitiveness and desire to be in the lead, thus working strongly against his other intention. You will see that this resolution has been entered in the next ring on the domain map.

In a way, though, as we have already mentioned, this is a relatively simple intention to work on. When you come to consider rather more major changes or courses of action, then you will almost inevitably find that these involve other people as well. And this is where we return to the difficulty of managing ME first; that although yes, self-management is the main thing, this needs to be done in full consciousness of the effects of what you do on other people. In that sense – making a conscious choice, taking into account the effects on others, and then *deciding* (rather than just drifting or being forced) what to do, you are behaving in a 'both —— and ——' way. Being prepared to be responsible for the consequences *both* for yourself and for others.

It may be that the probable consequences of a particular action are pretty clear, and you will be able simply to identify them and write them down. However, very often – especially with more complex issues and concerns – it's not as simple. In such cases, the method known as moral imagination is recommended.

Moral imagination

The title 'moral imagination' was given to this method by Rudolf Steiner; the use of the term 'moral' indicates that it involves bringing into your consciousness the consequences of your actions, both for yourself and for others – the other 'stakeholders' in your actions, who are involved and/or affected by it, and therefore who have an interest, a right to be considered. Of course, in the end it's *your* decision, although you may very well wish to consult them. But your decision will then be made in full consciousness of its effects – which often makes it harder, by the way. Awareness doesn't necessarily lead to comfort! At the very least you might then be able to consider ways of lessening the negative consequences for others, rather than just ignoring them or, in some ways worse still, being unaware of them. (Just as ignorance of the law is no defence for a crime, so in the moral sphere unawareness is no excuse. Indeed, it could be argued that morally, unawareness is the biggest sin.)

The technique is easier to describe than to do! It involves taking the possible course of action that you are evaluating, and imagining that you are now some time in the future, and that you did indeed make that particular choice. In other words, you have put that particular option into operation, and you are now imagining what has happened as a result. You will have to decide for yourself what time span to use; for a big decision you might try several – say one month, then six months, then one year.

It's important to be as detailed as possible in your imagination. Try to see what is happening, form a mental picture. Look for details such as colours, sounds, smells. What are you thinking? How are you feeling? What are you wanting to do, and actually doing? Who else is involved? What is each of them thinking? How is each of them feeling? What is each of them doing?

Although this may seem quite difficult at first, it is well worth persevering with. It's surprising how, using this method, you very soon realize that something you thought was a good idea isn't at all; or that you just haven't got enough information yet to make a proper choice or decision. Or that if you are to take such-and-such action, there are various other things you will need to do first; or you can do, in order to make it less unpleasant for some of the others involved.

For example, in the case of Peter's intention to change his lifestyle, he soon realized that option number 1 – stay at home and be a house-parent – wasn't for him. In his imagination he saw himself feeling frustrated and bored; and anyway, after quite a short time span the children had left home, so there was very little 'house-parenting' to do.

In fact, after doing moral imaginations and force-field analyses on the other alternatives, Peter came to his second resolution: to stay in his present job but change his attitude to it.

PLANNING FIRST STEPS

Many models of decision-making stress the importance of detailed action plans, which map out all the various steps that you are going to have to carry out, with target dates, criteria for measuring success, sub-plans for allocating resources, and so on.

Our approach is a bit different, since quite frankly we have often found that action-planning becomes a convenient vehicle for avoiding actually doing anything.

Instead, we like to focus on the *first step*; what is the *first* thing you are going to do? When? How? Once you have carried out that step, you can think about the next one; and so on.

It sounds simple, but of course there's more to it than meets the eye. You need to think about forthcoming opportunities – when will be a good or appropriate time to do something, to make a move and start implementing my resolution? And what can I actually do?

For Peter, his first resolution is relatively simple. He can start right now – or tomorrow evening, when he gets back from Edinburgh, when he will begin some of the exercises and meditations from Chapter 6 of this book. Even here, though, perhaps he needs to give a bit more thought to his timing. After all, it would be a good idea, bearing in mind he wants to share more with his family, to spend most of the evening telling Pat about his plan, as well as discussing the Edinburgh conference with her, rather than disappearing to do exercises and meditation. So he changes his mind – he'll start the day after tomorrow: the fitness exercises as soon as he gets home, and the meditation later in the evening, three hours after dinner.

His other resolution is more complex. What opportunity is about to come along for him to start with his new attitude? Well, he can cancel that trip to Paris – ask Janet to go instead. She'll probably be delighted, if a bit nervous, and it will be quite a developmental opportunity for her – provided Peter briefs her fully. . . . Well, not *too* fully; she's got to be given the chance to think for herself, and he must start trusting her, along with the others, to do so.

Sometimes, of course, it's relatively easy to plan a first step, and harder to carry it out. It can be extremely useful to *rehearse* what you are going to say to someone. Although you can do this rehearsal on your own – talking to yourself – it's very much better to do it with a partner or in a group, with someone role-playing the other person. This is an excellent way of clarifying what you are going to say and of building confidence and gaining the courage to get out there and say it. Another way of getting yourself ready psychologically is to use affirmations – 'I *can* do it' is a very simple one. We look at this technique in detail in Chapter 4.

Another excellent idea is to make a 'telepathic contract' with your speaking partner or with members of your support group. This involves you setting a time when you are going to carry out your first step, and the others agreeing to think of you at that time – send you 'telepathic support vibrations', as it were. We often use this with development groups that we work with, and it's amazing how helpful the receiver of the support finds it. 'Knowing you were all thinking of me enabled me to go in and tell my boss I thought she was wrong . . .'

Here is another means of preparation:

VISUALIZATION EXERCISE

First, get yourself relaxed (see Chapter 6 for a good relaxation exercise). Then choose the step or action that you are going to take.

Now imagine that you have taken the step; that is, create a clear mental picture of you and/or the situation as you want it to be. Suppose, for example, your goal is to be able to address a large group without being overcome by nervousness, and that your first step will be to speak at the sales conference next week.

Now imagine yourself, poised and confident, standing in front of the group and giving a wonderful presentation. Try and be as detailed as possible; include the audience, and look at the way they are enjoying and admiring your performance. Revel in your ability to give brilliant answers to their questions. Hear and enjoy their applause. Bask in the glory of thanks and praise afterwards.

Does this sound a bit far-fetched? Well, try it. And how many times has the opposite 'worked' – i.e. you have tortured yourself with images of failure, to find them coming only too true!

DOING AND REVIEWING

The most important thing to say about doing is – DO it! Get on with it; carry out your first step.

Of course, as we have already noted, it's not always as easy as that. What happens when your courage fails you? Or when your willpower deserts you?

Well, first of all, remember your resolution, why it is important to you. If you did a rehearsal, remember what you learned from that.

Think of others who are supporting you – your speaking partner or support group. (On a recent follow-up to a workshop that we ran, Albert, one of the members, said that he felt he *owed* it to the other group members, who had helped him come to his resolution, to carry out his first step; this had sustained him when otherwise his courage would have failed.)

If you made a 'telepathic contract', carry that thought with you – sense the support coming your way. And what of other sources of 'supersensible' support? If your spiritual beliefs include the existence of other beings (Guiding Angels, God[s], whatever your preferred term is), can you look to them for support or guidance? Or what about your inner friend – that inner voice that, if you will allow it, will tell you what to do, how to do it. How in touch with *it* are you? (If you find difficulty in hearing such inner voices, then an excellent way of tuning in to them more effectively is through the exercise known as 'backwards review' – Chapter 3 – and/or by using some of the meditation exercises given in Chapter 6.)

Returning back inward, while you are carrying out your first step, try to be *aware* of yourself and what you are doing. Observe yourself objectively – as though you were watching someone else. Try to look out for things like:

Physically: How is this person (i.e. you; putting it in the third person can help with the necessary degree of objectivity)? Tense or relaxed? Still or fidgeting? Breathing shallow and rapid, or deep and slow? (It's no coincidence that we say, 'I took a deep breath and got on with it.')

Thinking: What are this person's thoughts, ideas, assumptions, here? Why? Where are they coming from? Where are they going to? What effect are they having?

Feeling: How is this person feeling? Why? Where are these feelings coming from? Where are they going to? What effect are they having?

Willing: What would this person like to say or do? Why? Where is this coming from? What is her motive behind it? What ideally does he really want to do? What is she in fact prepared to do? Why?

What is he not prepared to do? Why not? What effect is all this having?

And, of course, it's not a bad thing if you can become aware of what the other people involved are thinking, feeling and willing! We'll look at that again in Chapter 7, when we examine the way you can work with others.

Through all this, remain aware of what's happening. You need to keep a fine balance between, on the one hand, not giving up or being thrown off course, and on the other hand realizing when you are getting nowhere, or making things worse, so that a change of plan is the best thing to do.

The way we have described it, then, the reviewing process actually starts during the doing. However, afterwards it will certainly be helpful if you take a more calm, detached look at what you did, how you did it, what happened, what you can learn from it. For this, methods such as backwards review (to which we have just referred, and which is described in Chapter 3) and critical incident analysis (also in that chapter) are very useful. Go and talk over this with your speaking partner or support group.

It may be that you see your resolution in a new light, or that you now recognize other key issues, or domains for mapping out action. But make sure you are not simply shying away from the original one. Conversely, don't be lulled by early success into thinking, 'That's it!' Don't forget this was only your *first* step. So, once you have reviewed it, you are ready for your *next first step*. And so the cycle continues.

COURAGE AND WILLPOWER

Finally, courage and willpower. Since these are particularly important when carrying out actions, you might like to try some simple exercises for strengthening them.

Improving your courage and willpower is a bit like improving your muscles – the more you use them, the stronger they get. Thus, if you find an activity that requires an effort of will to do it regularly, and are actually able to do it, then your willpower will improve.

A number of the activities described throughout this book are of that nature; for example, backwards review certainly calls on strength of will to carry out regularly.

SPECIAL WILLPOWER EXERCISES

We can divide these into two types – some that require an effort of will actually to do; and others where the act is quite easy, but the will comes in trying to do them every day.

Some examples of the first type include:

- When you are tempted to say something, hold back, don't say it.
- When you want to do something immediately – don't; postpone it instead, to a definite, specified time in the future.
- Conversely, when you want to postpone something – don't; do it right now instead.
- Do something that you know you don't want to; this needn't be particularly significant in itself – for example, you could deliberately not put sugar in your tea; or order a bacon sandwich when you would actually prefer a hamburger, or a vegetarian dish when you are longing for a hunk of meat.
- Still on food – order something you've never had before but think that you won't like.
- Talk to at least one complete stranger every day.
- Back to food – go to a restaurant and ask if it's possible to have something that's not on the menu.
- Think of some situation(s) that you would normally avoid and then put yourself in one of them – e.g. complain (as constructively as possible) about poor service, or unsatisfactory goods.
- Wear bizarre clothes for a day.

The second type of activity is a bit different; here the will-power comes from setting yourself a daily task or routine that you must stick to – preferably at the same time each day. The actual activity is more or less immaterial, although examples include:

- going for a short walk
- rotating a ring on your finger
- transferring a coin or other object from one part of your handbag (or one pocket) to another

3 Knowing yourself

In Chapter 1, we saw (Figure 1.5) a way of looking at ourselves that involved four aspects – our health, skills, action and identity. As we stressed, these are all interconnected, as they each depend on the other three.

For example, if we turn now to identity, it is clear that my sense of me, of myself, is very dependent on my health, skills and things that I do. At the same time, of course, the converse is also true.

In this chapter, then, we are concentrating on the *identity* aspect of Table 1.1, reproduced here as Table 3.1.

Table 3.1

Aspects of the self that require managing	Inner processes that require managing		
	Thinking	*Feeling*	*Willing* or *doing*
Identity, self	Personal values, ethical and moral standards, and philosophical, spiritual and/or religious beliefs. Awareness and understanding of these and other aspects of self. Thinking about myself and knowing myself.	Recognizing my strengths and rejoicing in them; accepting myself in spite of my weaknesses. Valuing myself.	Self-motivation, purpose in life; sense of security faith and hope. Being myself.

KNOWING, VALUING AND BEING MYSELF

To start with, let's look at the last words in each of the Thinking/
Feeling/Willing columns – namely *Knowing, Valuing* and *Being
myself*.

As we noted in Chapter 1, right from early schooling we are
taught about *other* people, what makes *them* behave, what
motivates them, what they did and achieved; their ideas, theories
and explanations. We are rarely encouraged to think for or about
ourselves, to find out about *our own* strengths, weaknesses,
actions, achievements, effects on others, etc.

Similarly, we are often taught that other people know more than
we do; that others are cleverer, better educated, more attractive,
nicer people – in short, that we should devalue ourselves relative
to others. And even when we are not actually being told these
things by parents, teachers, bosses and other authority figures, it's
all too easy for us to put ourselves down, to form a bad self-image,
whenever we do something not as well as we would like, receive
criticism, and so on.

That's not to say that criticism isn't desirable – indeed, in order
to know ourselves better, it is essential to receive both positive and
negative feedback. However, it is the way in which we receive it
that's important, and what we do with it. So, can I use negative
criticism as an opportunity for growth and development, or am I
going to allow it yet again to convince me how useless, unattractive, incompetent, etc. I am? (We come back to this later in
this chapter.)

Finally, we are often discouraged or indeed prohibited from
being ourselves. Others (parents, teachers, bosses) are usually
keen to make us into images of them – do it the way they tell you;
do it the way we've always done it here; behave in the 'right' or
'proper' manner. *Conform!!*

FIRM PUTS A BAN ON BEARDS

By CON COUGHLIN

The 'Corporate philosophy' of a Dallas-run computer company which forbids the wearing of beards and lunchtime drinking has erased the festive spirit at its newly-acquired British subsidiary, Unilever Computer Services.

The 200-strong workforce in North London have been told to abide by the 'code of ethics' of Electronic Data Services which decrees that men with beards must shave them off.

Moustaches are allowed providing they are neatly trimmed but casual clothes are strictly forbidden as is discussing your pay packet with friends and colleagues.

Helping to identify

Women must wear tights at all times and dress in blouses and skirts and must not under any circumstances wear trousers.

The edicts have left many of the workforce disgruntled. One employee said: 'It's appalling.'

But the company defended its clean-cut image yesterday, saying its 'code of ethics' was generally welcomed by the workforce and helped people to identify themselves with the company.

A spokesman for TASS, the computer union, said the Dallas code was an erosion of union rights.

(*Daily Telegraph*, 20 December 1984)

In fact, the same MSC-sponsored research that was referred to earlier has shown that managers go through a number of stages of development, during which they do move towards trying to think, feel and act for themselves – i.e. in a direction of greater self-management. (Each stage is characterized by particular ways of making decisions, related to levels of awareness, and therefore we also refer to the stages as 'modes of managing'.) Before summarizing these stages or modes, you might like to think about where you are, by completing the following questionnaire.

QUESTIONNAIRE ON STAGES/MODES OF MANAGING

Below are fifty statements about yourself and/or the way you manage. For each statement, allocate points as follows:

1 point   if it is completely untrue of you; you never think, believe or behave in that way

2 points if it is somewhat true of you; you sometimes think, believe or behave in that way

3 points if it is quite like you; you quite often think, believe or behave in that way

4 points if it is very much like you; you think, believe or behave in that way most of the time

At the end of the statements (page 68) you will find a table made up of boxes. Each box contains the number of one of the statements 1–50; write the points that you have scored yourself for that item (i.e. 0 to 4) in the appropriate box.

1 I base decisions on established rules and regulations.

2 I try to keep reasonably well-in with the powers that be.

3 I think that I have a contribution to make to the way that things are done around here.

4 I keep open-minded and take into account any views that other people may have, especially those that seem to differ from or contradict my own.

5 I feel that I know the answer to the question, 'Why on earth am I here?'

6 I don't think you should allow feelings to affect the way you do things.

7 I try to find out about the way we do things – who decided it, when and why.

8 A manager's job is to manage.

9 I try to ensure that I have an accurate picture of how others see me.

10 I am committed to a particular idea or philosophy of life.

11 When I am doing something unpleasant, I try to switch off my feelings and wishes and just concentrate on the established rules or procedures.

12 I like to have an explanation of the way we do things.

13 I base decisions on logical, rational thought.

14 I have a strange feeling that everything and everybody are somehow connected.

15 There are some issues and principles to which I am prepared to give priority over my own personal success and ambition.

16 I like to do things by the book.

17 I like to become really proficient in certain specific areas – 'our resident expert on . . .'

18 I go to others for their opinions, and then take these into account when coming to my own decision.

19 You should take feelings as well as facts into account when making decisions.

20 I wonder if I'm making a really useful contribution to the world.

21 When something goes wrong, or I make a mistake, I'll either refer back to the procedures or ask for instructions.

22 If I didn't agree with what was expected of me, I would still do it rather than risk rocking the boat.

23 I like to think things out for myself rather than rely on other people's decisions or explanations.

24 When making decisions, I try to put myself in the place of the other people who are involved and affected and imagine how they will feel.

25 I know what it is that I have to give to the world.

26 I'm at a loss when something new or unexpected turns up.

27 I think that you've got to be clear-cut and decide things one way or the other.

28 I am developing my own way or style of doing things.

29 I base decisions on intuitive feelings for what's involved.

30 I have a degree of dedication to some more important cause than my own development.

31 A manager's job is to issue instructions and see that they are carried out.

32 I sometimes have ideas that I think wouldn't be acceptable around here, so I keep them to myself.

33 I look for new experiences, even though these may be difficult and involve uncertainty and risk.

34 A manager's job is to enable everybody to manage themselves.

35 I'm prepared to make personal sacrifices for something I feel to be very important, other than my own career or development.

36 I look to others for instructions as to what to do.

37 When a change occurs I go to others who are also involved and ask them what they are going to do.

38 When something goes wrong, or I make a mistake, I try to learn from it and decide what to do next time.

65

39 I place importance on thinking about what I can do for my subordinates' development as well as for my own.

40 A manager's job is to create a better world for others to live in.

41 I like to have clear-cut guidelines.

42 I find myself wanting to challenge the status quo but don't bother because there's no real point and it will only make life difficult.

43 Sometimes I feel as though my face no longer fits around here.

44 When I am doing something, I am aware of the effect that my own feelings, wishes and prejudices are having on me, and try to take this into account before coming to a final decision.

45 I believe that I have a real contribution to make to society.

46 When I have finished this questionnaire, I would like to be given an interpretation of my score with instructions on what it means and what I should do about it.

47 When I have finished this questionnaire, I would like to compare my scores with those of other people.

48 When I have finished this questionnaire I would like the opportunity to think about what my scores might mean.

49 When I have finished this questionnaire, I would like to think about it in conjunction with what I have gathered about myself from other methods described in this book and elsewhere.

50 When I have finished this questionnaire, I would like to think about what it means in terms of the extent to which I am able to make a useful contribution to society.

Scoring table

	1	2	3	4	5
	6	7	8	9	10
	11	12	13	14	15
	16	17	18	19	20
	21	22	23	24	25
	26	27	28	29	30
	31	32	33	34	35
	36	37	38	39	40
	41	42	43	44	45
	46	47	48	49	50
TOTAL					
STAGE	1	2	3	4	5

What, then, does this tell about you as a manager?

When people first become managers they are usually reasonably happy to obey the rules, use standard procedures, use standard checklists and so on, as this gives them a secure basis from which to start (stage/mode 1). Then, after some time they become skilful at sussing out the unwritten rules too, the norms, accepted practices, conventions, reasons and explanations (stage/mode 2). This is shown at the start of Table 3.2. Still looking at the table, you see that although quite a number of managers are happy to stay like this – to flow with the tide and remain controlled by these external factors – sooner or later those who are more effective, who achieve more, move on to the next stage of their development, by adding another mode of managing to their repertoire. This is when they start to want to think for themselves, to change things, to try out their own ideas, and these are the people who are more flexible, and able to manage in times and situations of crisis and change.

Unfortunately, this may well bring them into conflict with those who prefer to stick to the established ways of behaving and doing things. Sometimes, of course, there's a good reason for the latter, but all too often bosses do stop new ideas for most inappropriate reasons. (Of course, in your role as boss etc., you will not be immune to this fault! As we stress in Chapter 6, keeping an open mind is an important aspect of healthy thinking.)

There is a danger, though, that the independent thinker's enthusiasm and self-confidence might well get in the way of their objectivity, and a certain degree of arrogance often creeps in. This needs to be tempered with humility, which comes from realizing that other people have legitimate ideas, opinions and rights.

So, as you get wiser – more aware – you learn to take a broader perspective. This will involve suspending judgement, keeping an open mind, listening to others, taking a 'both —— and ——' approach, getting feedback about yourself and your ideas, and considering the wider effects of your proposals, not only on yourself or your department, but also on others.

Although presented as a clear progression, it's not always quite so easy to recognize where you – or someone else – are at. For example, many managers become incredibly adept at recognizing the 'tricks of the trade' – the little things (like how not to show that you can't remember somebody's name) that really are somewhat manipulative. When carried out with consummate ease these may give the impression that the individual concerned is operating in a stage/mode 3 manner – having thought these things out for themselves. Really, however, this is not the case. For what we are seeing here is not true thinking, but an extremely subtle mixture of trial and error and ability to suss out norms, i.e. somewhere between stage/modes 1 and 2. So this is the area that Dale Carnegie specialized in – 'How to Win Friends and Influence People' – without the need for thought (mode 4) or real human contact and empathy (mode 5). A more modern, managerial version of this is to be found in the best-selling *One Minute Manager*; the fact that it does sell so well shows the longing that so many managers have for something that will unstick them. Unfortunately, since they are indeed stuck at mode 1 or 2, a mode 1 or 2 simplistic solution isn't going to be at all helpful in the long term; very soon they will come across the rest of us, who delighted in reading the aptly named riposte, *The 59 Second Employee* (which is, of course, another set of tips and tricks to counteract the first: again, no real understanding, contact or exploration of other people's positions).

You will see that this is all summarized in the table, which ends with a further stage or mode, when some people, if not all, feel a need to use this maturity for a definite, identifiable purpose. Perhaps these are in the minority; certainly the research showed that most managers normally behave between modes 2 and 3, and in these terms one of the intentions of this book is to look at ways in which you can consider your own stage of development and take your next step forward.

There is, in fact, a lot in this particular table. We suggest that you take time to read and re-read it; think about it; discuss it with a partner or in a group. You won't be able to do it justice if you just skim through it!

Your score from the questionnaire should give you a profile as to your repertoire of modes of managing. (The higher the score,

Table 3.2

Developmental stage or mode	Benefits of this way of managing	Effect of being blocked at this stage	Nature of next developmental step
1 Rules and procedures	Set procedures etc. can be of use in certain types of emergency, where it is particularly important to do the 'right' thing quickly and correctly. They are also useful for beginners, because they can provide a reassuring base from which to start.	In fact, not many managers are stuck at this stage. Those that are can only operate in a limited number of 'standard' situations, and are likely to be most ineffective at anything that might be described as 'truly managerial'.	To move on, you need to start querying, modifying or deviating from standard procedures, seeking explanations and reasons rather than mere instructions.
2 Norms and conventions	Enables you to behave in an 'appropriate' way – i.e. in the way that is in accord with accepted reasons, rationales and explanations, and is socially and politically respectable. In so doing you are likely to be popular with the powers that be, keeping your nose clean and being considered safe, acceptable and reliable.	Many managers remain at this stage, and are quite happy to do so, since it can lead to a reasonably content existence. On the other hand, these managers are likely to find any unexpected change most unpleasant and difficult to cope with. Should they be forced to leave the organisation (e.g. through redundancy) they will have a particularly bad time adjusting to their new situation. Also, of course, there is often a long-term price to be paid for not being oneself – a certain malaise, doubt, 'surely there's more to life than this?' begins to creep in. They suffer from all the effects of not managing themselves that were outlined in Chapter 1 – i.e. they are stuck, become bored, lazy, timeservers etc.	You need to start questioning and challenging the established and accepted ways and reasons for doing things. Start to think for yourself: do you really think this is the best way of doing something? Is this really a good, acceptable or valid explanation or reason? How can you find out for yourself, come to your own conclusion or decision?
Influenced mainly by external factors			

70

3 Thinking for yourself *Enter the self: now internal factors have a big influence*	Much more likely to be creative, and to be able to manage new, ambiguous, changing situations, both within your organization and in other aspects of your life. Also greater feelings of self-confidence and self-worth. The price to pay for this is that you may well be unpopular at times with those who like to maintain the status quo and do things in the 'proper' manner.	Being stuck at this stage means that you are so keen on thinking for yourself that you become too self-directing, completely ignoring the ideas, feelings, values and goals of other people, and the effect of your actions on them. You are also likely to distort your confidence into a form of arrogance.	You need, therefore, to start to temper your arrogance with humility, and to synthesize or combine self-management with management by and of other people; particularly by becoming aware of their views etc., and of the effect of your actions on them before coming to your final decision. It is also useful at this stage to start thinking about what you have to offer others, to contribute to their development.
4 Awareness *Now it's both internal and external factors, in a synthesis of the two*	You are now thinking for yourself, making your own decisions etc. in full awareness both of yourself and of others and their goals, ideas, feelings; this leads to what is often seen as 'intuitive behaviour'. To do this involves '... both ... and' thinking, and requires open-mindedness and suspension of judgment; in addition, of course, this awareness enables you to choose which of these modes to operate in – i.e. you now have a repertoire available to you, from which you can choose consciously. Thus, this is the stage of effective management, as outlined in Table 1.1.	Not a bad stage to be 'stuck' at! However, you may now find an increasing need and desire to use these skills, this ability to manage yourself, to a particular purpose, that you yourself feel to be important. There is also a danger of abusing these abilities, this high level of consciousness, to further personal ambition, manipulate others and gain power over them, or for other negative, evil ends.	Start to look for this special purpose; ask, 'Why on earth am I here? What am I doing with my life?'
5 Purpose *Now you apply this synthesis, this art of managing yourself, to a particular purpose – to your purpose in life*	Now you are managing yourself with a full awareness of your purpose in life, of the task you want to achieve. Hopefully this task isn't something just for yourself, but in some way makes a definite contribution to the development of your organization, profession, area of expertise, community, affinity group, family, or whatever it is that you choose to commit yourself to. However, there is also a great danger that this commitment will be to some negative or evil cause – this is where we find fanatics, despots, tyrants (sometimes obvious, sometimes posing as great saviours).		

71

the more you are operating in that way.) It is now up to you to decide what you think of this, how you feel about it, what you want to do about it, bearing in mind what the table says about the good and bad aspects of each mode, and the sort of things you can do to start to move into the next one. There is certainly information coming your way here, to feed into the action-process that we have described in Chapter 2.

However, it should by now be apparent that this book is intended to enable you to increase your awareness, to *move towards* stage/mode 4 or perhaps even 5. It's not so much that stage/mode 4 behaviour is always better than 1 or 2, but rather that in order to manage yourself fully you need to be able *consciously* to select or call on the mode that seems most appropriate at any given time. To manage yourself you need to be able to weigh up the situation, decide which mode to use, and go ahead in that way.

KNOWING YOURSELF

We will come to *Valuing* yourself and *Being* yourself in the next chapter. Here, we will concentrate on the first of those three aspects of one's sense of identity – namely *Knowing* yourself.

What a vast topic! Perhaps it's being overambitious to try to know everything about yourself – it would, quite literally, take a lifetime. (Although if you have worked through this book so far you should already have increased your self-knowledge quite a bit.) So what we will do here is to describe a number of methods that you can use for gaining more self-knowledge, both now and whenever you want to have another go at it in the future. The jargon phrase we use for this is 'getting feedback'.

Receiving feedback constructively

Before we go into this, try this little exercise.

Think of the last three or four occasions when you were given the opportunity of learning something about yourself. What did you do? Did you run away from the situation? If so, how did you do so, in what manner? And why?

Or did you stay with it? If so, how did you respond to the information, and to its source? Constructively or negatively?

In each case, what was the end result? What was the effect on you and your development and self-management? And on the other people involved?

Much depends on how you respond to feedback. Figure 3.1 summarizes the main things that tend to happen; how does this compare with your experiences that you have just been recalling? One of the problems about receiving feedback, of course, is that you may not like what you get; negative information about oneself is never particularly pleasant to receive!

Because of this, many of us tend to avoid opportunities for getting feedback. Similarly, when we do get information about ourselves, if we don't like it we resort to a number of ways of not taking it in. These include denial ('It's not true'); flight ('I must go to the loo'); rationalization ('It doesn't matter because . . .'); shifting the blame ('It was all because somebody else . . .'); attacking the source ('That person's an idiot anyway'); and subtle combinations of these and other ways of dodging the issue. What's your favourite?

If you feel that the criticism is – or might be – justified, do try to listen; don't deny, attack or run away, but take the risk of drawing the person out, prompting for more, seeking clarification. 'Have there been other times when you felt that I insulted you?' 'Can you tell me more about just what it was I did that you found un-acceptable?' 'Can you give me an example of the sort of behaviour you are talking about?' 'What was it I said that upset you?'

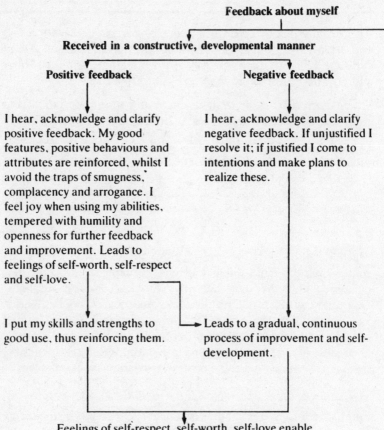

Feedback about myself

Received in a constructive, developmental manner

Positive feedback   **Negative feedback**

I hear, acknowledge and clarify positive feedback. My good features, positive behaviours and attributes are reinforced, whilst I avoid the traps of smugness, complacency and arrogance. I feel joy when using my abilities, tempered with humility and openness for further feedback and improvement. Leads to feelings of self-worth, self-respect and self-love.

I hear, acknowledge and clarify negative feedback. If unjustified I resolve it; if justified I come to intentions and make plans to realize these.

I put my skills and strengths to good use, thus reinforcing them.

Leads to a gradual, continuous process of improvement and self-development.

Feelings of self-respect, self-worth, self-love enable me to respect, value and love others. This and the resultant ability to manage myself lead to mutually enhancing and developmental relationships with other people in my family, friends, community, organization, etc. Positive spiral of two-way feedback.

Figure 3.1

Received in a non-constructive, regressive manner

Positive feedback

Negative feedback

I become proud, smug, complacent. Alternatively, I don't in fact hear positive feedback, or I deny it, or play it down, with overriding bad or negative self-image and feelings about myself.

My negative feelings about myself are reinforced; and/or I feel threatened and insecure and therefore ignore or deny the feedback, often attacking or running away from its source.

I continue to avoid other opportunities for change, improvement and development, preferring to remain stuck with an unrealistic sense of my own brilliance, and/or resting on my laurels rather than facing up to new challenges.

I continue to refuse to look at my negative aspects in order to improve. Subconsciously I am probably dimly aware of these, and therefore I grow to dislike, despise or hate myself. Often this is accompanied by an urge for self-destruction, and an inability to find, recognize and use the strengths that I do in fact possess.

Certainly no development. Indeed, my combination of smugness and self-hatred, coupled with my consequent inability to manage myself, probably lead to regression and even damage or destruction to myself, family, relationships, organization or community.

75

Of course, sometimes the criticism is indeed unjustified. Nonetheless, the person giving it to you must have some reason. If you hope to build or maintain a useful relationship with that person you will find that in the long term it will pay you not simply to ignore or dismiss such unjustified feedback, but to clarify and tackle it.

To start with, it doesn't help to deny the criticism, nor to get on the defensive, nor to counter-criticize back. Instead, listen carefully, and try to see where the criticism is coming from. Is this the final result of something you did quite a long time ago? (In which case it is in a sense justified, but you need to clarify the real cause and then explore that.) Or are you actually catching it in the neck for somebody else, or because you are at the end of a long day of frustration, worry, feelings of threat, or what have you? If so, you will have to decide whether to let it pass or confront it: 'Look, Yashwan, it seems to me that you are worried about tomorrow's meeting, and that's getting in the way here. Can we leave this for the time being, and is there anything we can do together now that will make you feel more confident about tomorrow?'

Perhaps you can see why the other person feels as they do about you or what you've done, even though overall you don't agree with their interpretation or criticism. In a case like that, it's useful to show you do have some understanding – although only go as far as you feel comfortable doing. 'Perhaps I should have let you know sooner'; or 'It could be that in my enthusiasm I acted too quickly and forgot to consult you.'

It's also very easy to receive positive feedback in a non-constructive way. Lots of people refuse to hear good things about themselves, and deny these, or trivialize them, or don't really believe them ('You're only saying that to be kind').

So try to learn to accept praise graciously. Hear it, recognize it, acknowledge it: 'Yes, I am pleased with the way I was able to put my case'; 'Thank you, yes I think that I did do a good job that day.'

On the other hand, it's possible to be so taken with good news that you become smug, full of your own brilliance, and thus blind to other aspects of yourself. People who are like this often engage in mutually sycophantic relationships, always giving each other unjustified praise, and avoiding any form of potentially constructive criticism. Another variant of this, of course, are the bosses or leaders who surround themselves with yes-persons; we all see a lot of that about these days.

SELF-KNOWLEDGE THROUGH FEEDBACK

In everyday life, if you want to know, for example, how your hair is looking, you either use a mirror or ask somebody.

This, then, is the basic process of finding out about yourself – you need something, or somebody, to act as a mirror.

Other people are so important in developing your ability to manage yourself that we are devoting a special chapter (Chapter 7) to the subject. Here we will concentrate on other types of 'mirror'.

Perhaps we should repeat what we said in the Introduction, that in no way are we suggesting that you do all of these activities at one go; you'd become totally exhausted! Remember, we are trying to provide a variety of methods, so that you can choose a few that appeal to you at that particular time.

MIRROR, MIRROR ON THE WALL

In fact, looking in a real mirror might be quite a good way of starting to learn more about yourself. Sit or stand in front of a mirror – the longer it is, the better – with or without clothes on. Have a really good look at yourself – all too often we try not to see ourselves too carefully.

First, look at your physical self; how is your body looking? How do you feel about it? Ask various parts of it how they are getting on, what they would like from you, how they would like to be treated. Although this may sound a bit weird, give it a try – and allow time for you to 'hear' what they say. (We are not implying here that parts of your body can actually speak to you; the point is that in your subconscious you almost certainly know what's needed – but usually we are so busy with noise and action that we just never hear what our subconscious is trying to tell us.)

Ideally, before moving on just jot down your reactions so far. Then move on to think about your skills. Again, look at the image in the mirror and say, 'This is a person who is skilful at ——; on the other hand, it would be useful if she improved her skills at ——' As before, jot down the answers.

Next, still looking at your reflection, think about what you do in the world. 'This is a person who has achieved ——, and is currently doing, or about to do, —— Nonetheless, it would be helpful and useful if he were to get out and ——'

Finally, 'What makes this person unique, special, is her ——. As a result, she feels —— about herself.'

Obviously, you may want to put quite a lot into the blank spaces above.

The prime purpose of this mirroring exercise is to get a better picture of yourself. At the same time, of course, you may have triggered off feelings (positive or negative) about yourself; if you want to explore these feelings further, and get some ideas about ways of working with them, you will find a number of ideas in Chapter 4. Don't forget, too, what we have said about planning and implementing action, back in Chapter 2.

BACKWARDS REVIEW

This is a very basic and fundamental exercise for becoming more aware and conscious of yourself. You can do it at any time, although towards the end of the day is most logical.

iderFind a quiet place to sit (you can do this exercise lying down, but it will very likely send you asleep; this might be good if you are suffering from insomnia, but isn't its real purpose!). Then go through the events of the day, in your imagination, starting with the most recent, and working backwards. Try to recall what you did; indeed, visualize this if you can – try to *picture* what happened. What were you thinking at the time? How were you feeling? What did you want to do? What actually did you do? And what of the other people involved – what were they thinking, feeling, willing and doing?

At first you will probably find this quite a difficult exercise. If so, start by just going back over the past two or three hours, gradually extending it to cover the whole day. As a result you will gradually become much more conscious of yourself, how and why you behave, how you affect others, what effect they have on you.

To work properly, Backwards Review, like a number of the activities and exercises in this book, needs to be carried out regularly, every day, over a long period of time (such as the rest of your life). A more discrete, occasional activity is the analysis of critical incidents. By 'critical incident' we mean something that happened that had special significance for you; perhaps it was something that you think you handled particularly well – or badly; or when you felt hurt, or angry, or happy, or whatever. Obviously it's for you to decide.

There are various ways of analysing such incidents. The one we are suggesting here is through keeping a personal journal.

PERSONAL JOURNAL

Take a notebook and divide the page into two halves, as follows:

What happened	*My behaviour*
Note here what happened; who else was involved, what they did, and what you think they were feeling and thinking.	Write down your thoughts and feelings about this incident. What did you want to say and do? What did you actually say and do? (For a more detailed analysis you can use the self-observation checklist from the 'Action' section in Chapter 2.)

Let a bit of time elapse (say at least a day) and then read over the incident again. Looking at what happened, how do you feel about it now? What do you think of it? What does it make you want to do? Is there any unfinished business? What are you going to do? What have you learned from all this?

Over a period of time you will accumulate quite a number of incidents. You may then find it helpful to use a further technique for interpreting them, calling the Repertory Grid. This is what might be called an 'analytical mirror', as it provides an excellent way of looking deeper into information about yourself – i.e. into analysing that data.

REPERTORY GRID

Suppose you have recorded, over a period of time, a number of critical incidents, and you have begun to notice that a picture is emerging, in that there are clearly times when you have been able to manage yourself quite well, and others when this has unfortunately not been so. You now want to explore this further, to see if you can find out more about what happens in these situations.

The first step is to pick out about ten incidents for analysis. Ideally, half of these should be 'successful' ones, the other half 'unsuccessful'. Then identify or label each with a single word or very short phrase, so that you can refer to it later quickly and easily.

To illustrate this, we will take six incidents from Tom's journal; to help with the explanation we will simplify them a bit, but basically they are real happenings.

Brief synopsis of incident	*Brief label*
A terrible row in a shop, triggered off when they had sold out of something that had been widely advertised as on special offer.	Shop
A presentation to a group of managers to introduce them to the idea of joining a self-development group.	Presentation
A meeting with a sponsoring body to obtain funding for a proposed project.	Sponsor
An argument with the guard on a train because the buffet car that was shown in the timetable was not available due to 'operating reasons'.	Train
A lecture given to a group of management trainees.	Lecture
An altercation with a waitress in a restaurant because the allegedly 'fresh fruit salad' was from a tin.	Restaurant

When you have selected and labelled your incidents, draw up a chart like that shown in Figure 3.2 and enter the labels of your

Characteristics	Incidents					
	Lecture	Shop	Train	Restaurant	Presentation	Sponsor

Figure 3.2

incidents along the top row, as illustrated. It doesn't matter which order you put them in. Now take each of the incidents and write its label on a separate small piece of paper. (So, for Tom's six incidents, six small pieces were used.) Shuffle these like a pack of cards, and select any three of them at random.

Take these three, and think about them in relation to each other. In our example the three were *Lecture*, *Train* and *Sponsor*. If possible, try to see if any two of the three are more similar to each other than the third one; i.e. in some ways they are alike, and the other is the odd one out.

For the three in the example, *Train* stands out as being different from the other two – it's the odd one out. Why? Well, to start with it was handled badly, while the other two were handled well.

So we note this in the 'Characteristics' column, by making a small scale (or construct, to use the technical term) of 'Handled well *vs* Handled badly', and noted down like this:

L   R

| Handled | Handled |
| well | badly |

The L and R just stand for 'Right' and 'Left'; it does not matter which end of the scale you put the descriptions – it would be just as valid to put 'Handled well' at the right-hand end with 'Handled badly' at the left.

Still considering these three, we notice that two were to do with work, while the other wasn't. Hence the next construct:

L   R

| Connected | Not connected |
| with work | with work |

You continue this process until you cannot see any more such sets of similarities/differences. Of course, the pairings won't

83

always be the same; for example, still using the same three incidents, I notice that the other people involved in *Sponsor* were all older than me, while for *Lecture* and *Train* they were either younger or the same age. This gives rise to the construct:

L	R
Other person(s) mostly older	Others mostly younger/same

(Again, it doesn't matter which one you put as L or R.)

Keep working away with the same three incidents, in various combinations of 2:1, until you think you have got out as many constructs as possible. Then return those three bits of paper to the pile, shuffle again, and select three more.

Suppose this time I come up with *Restaurant, Presentation* and *Sponsor*. (It doesn't matter that I've already had one of these – as long as they're not all three the same as a previous try.) At once, *Presentation* and *Sponsor* pair together on the 'Handled well *vs* Handled badly' dimension that I have already identified. However, I also notice a new one, in that I remember that with both *Restaurant* and *Presentation* I was feeling quite ill with a very severe cold, whereas with *Sponsor* I felt fighting fit. Thus we can now add another dimension:

L	R
I was feeling ill at the time	I was feeling well at the time

This process continues until you have either gone through most of the permutations/combinations of the three-at-a-time incidents, and/or until you have a total of about ten to fifteen constructs. (In our worked example, for brevity, we have stopped sooner than that.) You should then have a chart looking something like Figure 3.3.

Characteristics	Incidents					
	Lecture	Shop	Train	Restaurant	Presentation	Sponsor
L						
R						
Handled well						
Handled badly						
L						
R						
Connected with work						
Not connected with work						
L						
R						
Other person(s) mostly older						
Others mostly younger/same						
L						
R						
I was feeling ill at the time						
I was feeling well at the time						
L						
R						
I felt cheated. ripped off						
I did not feel that						
L						
R						
I had set up the situation (power)						
The situation just arose (powerless)						

Figure 3.3

85

What you now have, then, is a list of incidents and a set of your own *personal constructs* – i.e. a picture of the way *you* see things, think of them, perceive them. For example, I noticed the age factor in mine, even though at the time of the incident I might very well not have been conscious that I was aware of the people's ages. So at this stage it may prove rewarding for you just to look at your list of characteristics, dimensions, constructs, call them what you will, and ask yourself what you make of them. How do you feel about them? Are there any surprises? Do they give you any ideas for doing something?

A very interesting – although quite challenging – exercise is to select a number of incidents that all involved the same other person or people (e.g. your boss, a particular sub-ordinate, your partner) and then either discuss your grid with that person or, better still, work on it together. You might well get some very useful insights by comparing your constructs with theirs, for the shared incidents.

The constructs, then, tell you about how you perceive the world. You can take the exercise a stage further to see if you can find any insights into the way in which you respond to the world.

In the example this is shown in Figure 3.4.

You will see that we have 'scored' or 'rated' each of the incidents on each of the characteristics. So, looking at *Lecture*, I see this as having been handled well (thus L on the first construct); connected with work (L); involved people not mostly older than me (R); I was feeling well (R); I did not feel cheated (R); and I had set up the situation myself, thus feeling powerful in it (L).

Similarly, you enter R or L in all the other cases. (It is thus quite a crude scale – no 1, 2, 3, 4, 5 etc.; there are versions of repertory grids that use numerical scaling, but there's not much point unless you have various computerized ways of analysing these scores.) If you really don't think the construct applies at all to a particular incident, put a mark like an X or an

Characteristics	Incidents					
	Lecture	Shop	Train	Restaurant	Presentation	Sponsor
L Handled well / R Handled badly	R L	R	R	R	L	L
L Connected with work / R Not connected with work	R L	R	R	R	L	L
L Other person(s) mostly older / R Others mostly younger/same	R R	R	R	L	R	L
L I was feeling ill at the time / R I was feeling well at the time	R R	L	L	L	L	R
L I felt cheated, ripped off / R I did not feel that	R R	R	R	R	R	R
L I had set up the situation (power) / R The situation just arose (powerless)	R L	R	R	R	L	L

Figure 3.4

87

* or something to highlight that.

Finally, the analysis. What you are looking for is a pattern between rows in the grid. Before illustrating this, can you see anything emerging from the entries in Figure 3.4?

There are quite a number of rather clear patterns (we did say this was simplified for illustration purposes!). As a start, compare the first two rows:

```
L  R  R  R  L  L
```
and
```
L  R  R  R  L  L
```

In fact, they are identical. In other words, from this (slightly hypothetical) data, it seems that Tom is much better (L) at handling things at work (L), since he handles badly (R) things not connected with work (R).

That's an easy one to spot. Look now at the first dimension and the last-but-one – feeling cheated. These read:

```
L  R  R  R  L  L
```
and
```
R  L  L  L  R  R
```

These, then, are exact opposites. However, you will remember we have stressed that it doesn't matter which end you put the various characteristics; so if 'I felt cheated' had been at the R end (instead of the L), then they would have been identical. In other words, strange though it may seem at first sight, there is a perfect similarity between rows that are exact opposites.

So, in this case, Tom handled things well (L) when he did not feel cheated (R) (Lecture; Presentation; Sponsor). On the other hand, when he felt ripped off (L), he handled it badly (R) (Shop; Train; Restaurant).

Of course, the fact that there is this link does not in itself imply a cause as such. What Tom now has to do is to think about this carefully, look into it further, decide if there is a 'message' there somewhere, and, if so, what he is going to do about it.

Finally, let's compare the 'Handled well/badly' and 'Feeling ill/well' dimensions. These are:

L R R R L L
and
R R R L L ,R

There doesn't seem to be any pattern here; L is paired with R three times, R with R twice, L with L once. In other words, this seems quite random, so at the moment, anyway, there does not seem to be any relationship between how Tom handles things and how well he is feeling.

The repertory grid, then, provides a very powerful tool for looking further into your incidents, or indeed for gaining insight into the way you see, feel, respond etc. to all sorts of things. For example, instead of critical incidents you could have analysed people whom you like and don't like (writing their names across the top, and various aspects of them as the constructs). Or things you like/dislike (or find easy/difficult) about your job; or situations you avoid compared with those you seek out; or times you feel well compared with when you feel ill. In all these cases, highlighting a pattern can be a first step to taking decisions and doing something at which we have already looked, in Chapter 2.

THE USE OF QUESTIONNAIRES

One of the most common methods of getting information about people is through questionnaires. Lots of these are available, although, in line with the dependency-culture discussed in Chapter 1, most are designed to give some specialist or expert information about somebody else (such as in selection processes). Nonetheless, there is undoubtedly a use for self-questionnaires as a means of gaining self-knowledge.

Knowing Yourself

Questionnaires can be divided into two types – open- and closed-ended. The former consist of questions that require you to write in an answer in your own words, while the latter involve some form of ticking boxes, choosing from alternatives, ranking things in order of preference, and so on, leading to a numerical score; indeed, the exercise earlier in this chapter (page 63) took this form.

The problem with open-ended answers is that they need *interpretation*, which many people assume should be done by an expert. However, in tune with our philosophy of self-management, we believe that it is both possible and indeed desirable for managers to think about their own answers to such questions; to interpret them themselves – although, of course, it may also be a good idea to discuss these with a friend or colleague (Chapter 7).

You can indeed use open-ended questionnaires directly with somebody else by treating them as an interview or discussion guideline, asking each other the questions and discussing them as you go along. Again, Chapter 7 gives some guidelines on the process of working together with someone in this way.

You will find a number of such items throughout this book. For now, here is one around the theme of this chapter – i.e. knowing yourself. As you will see, many of these questions are pretty hefty, and you could spend a long time on them. As we have previously remarked, with this type of question it is often a good idea to mull over some of them for a day or two before attempting a formal reply. Certainly you may want to concentrate on one or two questions per discussion (with a partner or with yourself) and tackle some of the others later. *Manage it in the way that suits you best.*

OPEN-ENDED QUESTIONNAIRE/ DISCUSSION QUESTIONS ABOUT KNOWING YOURSELF

(a) Personal values, beliefs and standards

1 What are your basic beliefs about people, work, family life, politics, morals, your country/nationality/race, your sex, people of other nationalities, other races, the opposite sex?

2 What are your basic beliefs about religion, spiritual matters, life and death?

3 Have you always thought and felt like this, or can you see ways in which your beliefs and values have changed over a period of time? If so, were these changes sudden, or evolutionary?

4 If you have said that you don't have any beliefs about any of these, then think again. You almost certainly do, even if they are very subconscious – perhaps in the form of hidden assumptions.

5 This is particularly true if you are finding any of these questions make you feel uncomfortable. In that case, try to identify the source of the discomfort. Become aware of it, and then, if you wish, make a *conscious* decision not to explore that area if you don't want to.

6 If you really do think that you have no conscious beliefs in any area, how do you feel about that? What, if anything, would you like to do about it? What are you going to do?

7 Can you see any inconsistencies in your beliefs – i.e. do any of them contradict each other?

8 Where do your beliefs come from? What are they based on? Who or what influences you in deciding what is right and what is wrong?

9 How do your beliefs and values influence your thinking, your feeling, what you want to do, what you actually do?

10 Can you think of some situations when you did something in a way that went against your basic beliefs or values? What happened? How did you feel? Why did you do what you did?

11 Looking over your answers to these questions, do you think that other people would see you in the same way as you see yourself? Or perhaps some would, some wouldn't?

12 Finally, looking back over your answers to these questions, what do you think of them? What picture does this give you of yourself? How do you feel about that? What, if anything, do you intend to do about it? (By now it should go without saying that it is perfectly okay to say you are not going to do anything, provided that's a *conscious* decision, made with due consideration of the pros and cons etc. Remember, *you* are managing *yourself*.)

(b) Knowledge about yourself

13 Write a two- or three-page description of yourself, in the third person, as though describing somebody else; i.e., 'She is . . ., etc.' What aspects of yourself do you find easy/comfortable to describe? What about difficult, uncomfortable or unaware aspects?

14 Why not show this description to some colleagues, friends, family? See if they recognize you. You can attach some blank sheets and ask them to add their own views of you.

15 Finally, looking back over your answers to these questions, what do you think of them? What picture does this give you of yourself? How do you feel about that? What, if anything, do you intend to do about it?

Obviously, this whole book is much to do with knowing yourself, but hopefully you will find some of these specific exercises useful, doing them either on your own, with a partner or in a group. In the next chapter we will go on to look at ways of working on *Valuing* yourself and *Being* yourself.

4 Valuing and being yourself

In this chapter we will continue the exploration of one's self-identity, by moving on from *Knowing* yourself to *Valuing* and *Being* yourself. As a start, you might like to get a picture of the extent to which you are valuing and being yourself at the moment, by going through the following open-ended questions, either on your own or with a speaking partner (see Chapter 7).

QUESTIONNAIRE/DISCUSSION QUESTIONS ABOUT VALUING AND BEING YOURSELF

1 How do you feel about yourself, about your strengths, weaknesses, characteristics? About your body, your health? Your skills and abilities? What you do in the world?

2 Imagine that you have been asked to write a character reference for yourself. What would you say?

3 In what ways do your feelings about yourself affect you and what you do, what happens to you, what other people do? Can you think of examples?

4 Do you think other people know how you feel about yourself?

5 Do you have any sense of purpose in life – what it is you are here to do?

6 What are your 'God-given gifts', and how are you using them? For whose benefit?

7 Who or what influences you – what you do, the way you do it? Why not draw up an 'influence map', showing sources of influence on you. Are any of these pulling in opposite directions? How do you react to all this? How well are you managing yourself?

8 Do you think that other people would share this view of you? Or perhaps some would, some wouldn't? Who?

9 Now, looking back over your answers to these questions, what do you think of them? How do you feel about them? What are you going to do about them?

HOW TO FEEL BAD ABOUT YOURSELF NEARLY ALL THE TIME . . .

We have already, in Chapter 3, commented on the way that we often develop bad feelings about ourselves as a result of negative feedback, or by making comparisons with others who seem much more competent, clever, beautiful, or whatever. These bad feelings spill over into our lives in two ways. First, they create a self-fulfilling prophecy; since 'I'm no good, no one will like me', I avoid others, withdraw, put people off, so indeed they leave me alone, because I'm not exactly an attractive life and soul of the party.

Things then get worse, because even though part of me is telling me I'm no good, another part doesn't want to believe that. So instead of taking responsibility for the fact that it's my own behaviour that is causing people to ignore me, I blame them – it's because they are nasty, or stupid, or boring, or whatever. So they're not the sort of people I want to get on with anyway, and I'm better off ignoring and avoiding them.

And so the vicious circle continues. The others notice my standoffish behaviour, and are all the more likely to keep away, reinforcing both my negative view of myself and my rationalized negative view of them. And so on and so on and . . .

This pattern of behaviour is so common that there is a whole approach to psychotherapy based on understanding its more severe consequences. Called 'Rational Emotive Therapy' (RET), it was developed by an American psychiatrist called Albert Ellis, who worked with patients who were strongly hooked into depression and/or self-destruction.

. . . AND HOW TO BREAK OUT OF THIS DESTRUCTIVE CIRCLE

We are not suggesting that 'the thinking manager', for whom this book is intended, is in need of therapy. However, we can modify the principles of RET to help break out of the vicious circle that leads all of us to feel down, somewhat depressed, as though it's been a really bad day.

Ellis showed that we all have a tendency to hold certain beliefs or assumptions about ourselves and others that are irrational – there's no logical reason why we should hold them. For example, one such belief is, 'I *should* be perfectly competent in all respects.' Who says so? Where does this belief come from? As soon as you start to look at it you see that it is completely unreasonable. Nobody could possibly live up to it – even if our parents, teachers, bosses try to tell us it's true! However, as long as we hold to that assumption we are going to be unhappy quite often, since there are bound to be many occasions when our lack of total competence becomes clear.

The trouble is, we then start to label ourselves. Instead of saying, 'Oh well, I would like to have done that better, but at least I can learn from it', we stick on the label 'I AM AN INCOMPETENT PERSON'. Off goes the vicious cycle again!

So what we need to do is to throw off that label. Start by

recognizing that the assumption behind it is a load of nonsense, and replace it with a much more sensible belief.

Let's look at some of these irrational assumptions in turn.

Irrational assumption no. 1: **I MUST be perfectly competent in all respects**. Now there's a wonderful weapon for self-punishment! Nobody can be *perfectly* competent in *all* respects.

So what happens to the holders of this ludicrous vehicle for self-torture? Clearly, from day to day they experience evidence that they are not such paragons of skilful virtue; they fail to live up to this impossible ideal. As a consequence, they punish themselves, put themselves down, feel inadequate, and so on. Worse, they label themselves: 'I AM A FAILURE'; 'I AM USELESS'; etc. Things get so bad that even when they do do something pretty well, they don't recognize it! They feel they should have done even better. Or when someone gives them positive feedback, they don't hear it, or think, 'You're only saying that to be kind', or 'I was just lucky', or whatever.

To break out of the destructive effects of this assumption, then, you need to replace it with something like this:

'Nobody is perfectly competent at anything, let alone everything. However, like everyone else, I do have certain abilities, and can do certain things reasonably well. These things are ——'

I.e., think for a time and make a list of what you are indeed good at. Overcome any false inner modesty (which is actually one of your inner enemies trying to stop you from valuing yourself). Perhaps talk to some other people about this; if you contract to work with them seriously on ways of managing yourselves (see Chapter 7) you will soon overcome any embarrassment at asking to be told what you are good at.

'Of course, sometimes I will perform better than at others.

However, these less successful times are *not* failures – they are opportunities for looking at what happened and learning from it. Therefore I am *not* a failure – I am someone who is developing and learning to manage myself even more effectively.'

At this point you may find it particularly helpful to strengthen the power of this new, positive assumption about you and the world by using what is known as the *affirmation method*. However, we'll look at that later in this chapter, and return now to the next of the RET irrational assumptions.

Irrational assumption no. 2: **I MUST have the love and approval of others at all times**. Here's another guarantee of misery. For a start, what wins the approval of one person is quite likely to be disapproved of by somebody else, so you are either going to live in a state of tension, as though on a vibrating tightrope, or you are going to do things which some people won't approve of. In any case, if your behaviour is dictated by needs for approval, you're not exactly managing yourself, are you?

Similarly, but perhaps even more so, with love. You can never be yourself if all the time you are doing things either to 'win' love or to avoid 'losing' it; and anyway, as deep inside you know, love isn't like that. It's not a commodity that can be bought or won.

That being so, your attempts to win or buy it won't succeed – by the very nature of things they can't. However, your irrational assumption triggers off another of your inner enemies and tells you that 'There is something terribly wrong with me.' You get a new label: 'I AM UNATTRACTIVE'; 'I AM UNLOVABLE'; 'I AM HORRIBLE'. So on you go, off into another negative cycle of self-fulfilling prophecies, which actually makes your behaviour less attractive to others, so they do find it harder to like you, thus reinforcing your view of yourself as unlovable etc.

At the same time, another neat device that your inner enemy gets you to do is to blame it all on others. It's *they* who are unkind, uncaring, rejecting, unfair, and so on. Alternatively, there's a nice defence called rationalization: 'Those people are so boring, stupid, unattractive, wicked, . . . that I actually don't want them to like me anyway.'

So what positive assumption or view of life can you take here? Something like this:

'It is nice when people like, love or approve of me. However, there are bound to be times when that won't be so. So what? Does it really matter? What is more important, managing myself or doing things to win friendship? If they don't want to be friends with me, so be it. In fact, if anything it's their loss rather than mine. Anyway, lots of people do like, love or respect me, including ——'

Now think about this and list those people. Contemplate the list; what sort of people are they? What sort of a person must *you* be if people such as them actually admire, respect, like or love you? What is it about you that they like? Can you check that out with some of them?

'Furthermore, people who don't seem to like me are not bad, horrid or whatever. It takes all sorts to make the world.'

Again, this may well be a good time to use the affirmation method, which we'll look at later.

Irrational assumption no. 3: **I have a RIGHT to rely on others to give me what I want**. Nonsense! Not only have you no such right, but this belief is the very antithesis of self-management. And since you're not going to get everything you want from others, you are going to become disappointed, frustrated, angry with these other so-and-sos who won't cooperate with you. So you tell yourself that 'I AM UNLUCKY'; 'I AM ALONE AND HELPLESS'; 'I AM BETRAYED'; and you label everyone else as uncaring, unhelpful, selfish bastards or bitches.

What of the constructive view, then?

'There are many times when others cannot, will not, or indeed should not give me what I want. So what? I have no right to expect them to – I wouldn't like *them* always to be expecting me to give them what *they* want. In any case, it wouldn't be healthy to be so dependent. A mature person knows when to manage for themself, when to seek assistance, and how to cope if such assistance cannot be forthcoming.

'Of course, it's nice to know that there are times when I can turn to certain people and ask for help – knowing that they will do their best but that if they cannot help me they will feel free to say so and we will still remain on good terms. Such people include ——'

Now list some of these people and think about your relationship with them. What sort of demands do you make? Are these always reasonable? How do you feel when they are/are not met? What contributions do you make to their lives?

'People who can't or won't help or give me what I want have every right not to do so. They have their own lives to manage, their own pressures, deadlines, concerns.'

Irrational assumption no. 4: **My heritage, upbringing, childhood or other things that have happened in the past MUST continue to determine my feelings and behaviour.** In other words, it's all somebody else's fault, and there's nothing I can do about it; so there's no point even trying. 'I AM AND ALWAYS WILL BE STUCK – UNSKILFUL, UNATTRACTIVE, STUPID, ALONE, etc.'; 'I AM AND ALWAYS WILL BE DOOMED'; 'I CANNOT EVER CHANGE OR DO ANYTHING ABOUT IT.'

This is certainly a good one for getting you into a state of frustrated, depressed apathy – often combined with envy or spiteful jealousy of others who appear to have had an easy time of it. But what about all those people who seem to overcome terrific handicaps and setbacks to achieve all sorts of successes. So why not switch to:

'What I was born with, together with my upbringing and other experiences, certainly have contributed to who and what I am now. However, I am *not* stuck with this. First of all, I *can* change and develop if I want to; and secondly, I am *free* to make what I can of myself and all my characteristics. I can build on my strengths; try to get a sense of meaning from my life so far – capitalize on its fortunate aspects and transcend the unfortunate ones, by saying, "So what?" to them. And I can face up to the challenge of the life questions now coming my way.'

At this point you may be able to list some of the fortunate aspects of your life, and identify the challenges *now* coming your way. However, a very useful way of exploring this in more depth is the biography approach, and we will come back to that later in this chapter. Incidentally, if you start to work with others and share biographies, you will very soon discover that the 'silver-spoon' brigade nearly always have had their own problems and issues, many of which will probably put yours in the shade!

Irrational assumption no. 5: **Unhappiness is EXTERNALLY controlled.** Perhaps this is the core of all these. As long as you blame others, project your feelings on to them, punish them – and yourself – for *your* inability to take charge of yourself, to manage yourself, then you will remain blocked, stuck, unfulfilled, unfulfilling. Why not try this:

'Nothing in life is perfect. However, I *do* have power and freedom to choose one of the four positive ways to respond to an unpleasant or unsatisfactory situation. I can either:

    1 *Change the situation.*
or 2 *Change myself.*
or 3 *Leave the situation.*
or 4 *Decide to live with the situation.*

These, then, are some of the irrational assumptions or attitudes towards life that prevent you from managing yourself. Think about them. Do they ring any bells with you? Are any of them preventing you from true self-management? And if so, can you find a friend – either another person or an *inner* friend, the counterpart to your inner enemy who is whispering these destructive attitudes into your ears?

HIGHER AND LOWER SELVES

Inner friends and inner enemies

Let's look a bit more closely at this idea of inner friends and enemies. We have encountered them already a few times in this book. In Chapter 1 Peter Ford's inner friend was telling him why he was taking on too much; indeed, it could be said that his painful neck was a message from within, saying, 'Hold on, start to look after yourself better.' And he is aware of part of himself – the fighting, politicking inner enemy, who doesn't want him to take stock of himself and what he's doing. As we noted, Peter 'didn't like that part of himself very much'. So, in Chapter 2, we looked at the way he turned this message into resolutions, and then did something about it.

In Chapter 3 we looked at two ways of receiving feedback – constructively and destructively (Figure 3.1). Here again your inner friend and enemy are at work.

In anthroposophical psychology these inner beings are referred to as our 'higher and lower selves'. Each of us has both of these; at all times our higher self – our inner friend – is trying to give us information, feedback and other messages that will enable us to do what is right, to make the best decision, to find courage when it's needed. Some sportsmen have learned this – there is a whole approach to sports training known as 'the inner game'. This too lies behind a number of meditative approaches to development – the meditation allows us to listen to the subconscious, inner voice of our higher self. (And at the same time, to develop some of the 'super senses' that are necessary for really skilled behaviour – see Chapter 5.)

All too often, though, our lower self – our inner enemy – seems to speak more loudly, to offer more seductive blandishments! It's so much easier to run away from a necessary confrontation; to ignore painful feedback rather than face up to it; to shout and yell rather than ponder on the validity of the other person's point of view; to wait until tomorrow before giving up smoking.

An important aspect of knowing, valuing and being yourself, therefore, is becoming aware of both your higher and lower selves. The first – your inner friend, that part of you which can help you to manage yourself in a really positive and constructive manner – needs to be recognized, valued, listened to.

You also need to recognize your lower self, and try to deal with it. There are a number of broad strategies for this, depending on the nature of the beast. For example, some are very vulnerable to being seen or recognized. Merely identifying it – giving it a name, if you like – is sufficient to rob it of its powers (remember Rumpelstiltskin?).

Others thrive on your fear of them; as long as you are afraid of that part of you, or hate it (and hence yourself), they will get stronger. What they cannot stand is to be ignored, or laughed at. So a way of dealing with them when they pop up is simply to say, 'Sorry, not this time', and turn your back on them. Of course, this is easier said than done, and you may well find it much easier if you are able to discuss all this with somebody else (Chapter 7).

There are numerous fairy stories about monsters, frogs, beasts and so on that were transformed into princes or princesses by somebody who was able to overlook their hideous or frightening aspect and feel warmth, affection or love for them. The same is true of some types of inner enemy, since within them hides a positive quality, if we could only release it. For example, my spoilt child, who flies into a tantrum or sulks when she doesn't get what she wants, may also have other delightful childlike qualities, such as a sense of playfulness, wanting to be allowed into the world. Or the bore who goes on endlessly about his past experiences may, with some feedback and encouragement, become an interesting and entertaining raconteur.

The same is true of our higher selves; these often have a less pleasant side to them. Thus, the amusing wit can be degraded or distorted into hurtful sarcasm. Courage can become foolhardiness (playing 'last across the road'). Commitment can become fanaticism.

RECOGNIZING OUR HIGHER AND LOWER SELVES

It might be useful for you to try to identify some of your inner friends and enemies. This isn't too difficult, as often we are semi-subconsciously aware of them. So try to recall a number of occasions when either your higher or your lower self was in evidence. Often, of course, they were both there; what happened to each of them?

If you can't think of any such occasions offhand, go back over the incidents in your incident diary (Chapter 3), and see if that gives you some clues. A repertory grid of these will almost certainly help (again, see Chapter 3); alternatively, if you have been able to identify aspects of both your lower and higher selves, why not try a repertory grid to analyse these further – using episodes when each was brought out as the incidents? This will probably give you a lot of insight into the nature of these parts of you, who/what/when triggers them off, who/what/when strengthens them, who/what/when weakens them, and so on.

Finally, you might like to try something that comes from psychosynthesis, in the form of a visualization exercise.

Tune yourself in, as it were, by reading through some of your critical incidents, or thinking about some of your personal traits and characteristics. Then close your eyes, and imagine that you are looking at a blank cinema screen. Allow an image to form on the screen – an image of part of your inner self, i.e. an aspect of your higher or lower self. This image may take the form of a person, an animal, bird, other type of creature or being, or an inanimate object. Whatever it is, don't interfere with it in any way; just let it form. It may change its form of its own accord; that's fine, as long as you are not changing it yourself.

Then allow it to speak to you. Listen to what it is saying. Can you sense what it is thinking? Or what it is feeling? Or what it wants from life – what is its ambition? Above all, what does it want from you?

If you cannot sense these, then ask it. And, finally, ask it its name.

Then let it fade away.

Some people find this a very difficult exercise; perhaps no

image appears at all, or they cannot make any sense of what they do see. If that happens with you, don't worry; either forget it (some exercises are bound to be more appropriate for you than others) or think about it from time to time; perhaps have another go later.

For others this can be a very powerful experience. It may be that you find it disturbing; for that reason, this exercise is one that can very usefully be done with someone else – either in pairs or in small groups.

If you did get an image – or a series, if you repeat the exercise over a period of time – you may then wish to go on to this next supplementary exercise.

Choose one of the aspects of your inner self that you want to work on further. Close your eyes, and now imagine that you are standing with it in a field. In the distance is a range of mountains, and you set off to climb one of these, with your inner being as your companion.

As you make your journey, the terrain changes. Sometimes it is rocky and steep; at others there are grassy plateaux, with birds and flowers. Sometimes it is warm and pleasant; at others it gets cold, rains or snows, fog and mist close down.

When all these things happen, observe your companion. How does she/he/it react to the different conditions? What does it do or say?

Eventually you get to the top of the mountain. The view is breathtaking, and the sun comes out strongly, so that both you and your companion are bathed in warm, golden light. What happens now? How do you both feel about each other? What do you both want to do? What are *you* going to do?

THE AFFIRMATION APPROACH

We have already, in the previous section, mentioned the affirmation approach to valuing yourself, and we will now look at this in more detail.

We have said that one of the dangers of holding negative views of ourselves is that this leads to self-fulfilling prophecies. Marion, in the case study in Chapter 1, saw herself as being no good at interviews, and therefore performed badly at her interview.

Well, the good news is that this strong cycle of self-image being reinforced can be turned into positive use, by starting off with positive views of oneself. And it doesn't matter if at the moment you don't have a very positive view, as we shall now see.

The affirmation method was first used in France, in the early part of this century, where it was invented by Emile Coué, who called the method 'autosuggestion'. There are a number of variants, but the principle is simple. You decide on the positive view of yourself that you would like to be true, and then tell yourself, many times, that it *is* true. And, just as telling yourself 'I can't do such-and-such' leads you not to be able to, then telling yourself that you *can* do it leads to success. (Coué's famous affirmation, around which he built a highly effective therapy practice, was simply, 'Every day, in every way, I'm getting better and better.')

If that sounds too good to be true, you are probably right. Like any other method, affirmation needs certain conditions to work properly.

HOW TO USE THE AFFIRMATION METHOD

Although it is possible, in moments of excitement or crisis, to use a quick, instant affirmation (e.g., 'Yes, I *can* do this'), as a method it requires a regular disciplined application, at frequent intervals (ideally every day).

It's also necessary to know what sort of affirmation you are going to make. To do this, you need to decide what your goal is – what aspect of yourself or your life you want to improve.

This can be almost anything. For example, a better relationship with ——; to be stronger; more healthy (but be precise — what aspect of your health do you want to improve?); to gain courage, or willpower. To feel relaxed, or full of energy. To be able to accomplish some specific task; to be attractive; to feel good about yourself. The possibilities are endless. No doubt you will gain lots of ideas for goals by reading various other parts of this book. In general, *anything positive can be worked towards by the affirmation method.*

Once you have a goal, you can then use one of a number of affirmation techniques. We will just describe one here. We are not saying it is better than others — but there is only limited space here.

Right, then. Suppose your goal is higher self-esteem. Take a notebook, or a number of blank filing cards, and write out the following:

I, Janet, am more and more pleasing to myself every day.
You, Janet, are more and more pleasing to yourself every day.
She, Janet, is more and more pleasing to herself every day.

I, Janet, am beginning to like myself as a woman.
You, Janet, are beginning to like yourself as a woman.
She, Janet, is beginning to like herself as a woman.

In each case, write it out three times, in the first, second and third persons as above. This is because our current views of ourselves are formed by a mixture of what we tell ourselves, what others tell us, and what others say about us. For space reasons, though, we won't put all three from now on in this book.

I, ——, am becoming nicer every day.

I, ——, am becoming happier to be me every day.

And so it goes. Of course, you can be as specific as you like. Here are just a few more:

I, ——, am beautiful and lovable.

I, ——, am talented, intelligent and creative.

I, ——, am growing cleverer every day.

I, ——, have much to offer, and others recognize this.

I, ——, am getting slimmer every day.

I, ——, am getting on better with —— every day.

I, ——, have a really beautiful nose.

I, ——, have a lovely sense of humour that others appreciate very much.

I, ——, am beginning to forgive —— for ——.

I, ——, am getting over my disappointment at ——.

I, ——, am working on that report so that it will be finished by ——.

I, ——, am confident and can speak my mind clearly and confidently at meetings.

Notice that these affirmations are all written in a positive sense; there are no negatives. (Thus, *not* 'I am not tense any more', but 'I am relaxed'.)

The important thing is to write these out, putting in your name (and the names of anyone else involved) and using I, you, she/he, at least ten times, and then reading them out loud.

Remember 'mirror, mirror' in the previous chapter? Well, it may help if you look at yourself in a mirror when reading out the affirmations you have written. Alternatively, read them into a tape recorder, and then play them – in your car, in bed at night, or indeed to wake you up in the morning, with a cassette-timer device. After all, what a splendid way to start the day, hearing something wonderful being said about you!

As with so many activities in this book, you can usefully do this one together with a partner. You'll probably find it difficult at first – after all, we don't normally go around saying nice things about ourselves to others! However, your partner will be able to give you most helpful feedback about your posture, and the way you state your affirmation – whether or not it sounds as though you mean it. The point is, of course, to keep at it until you *do* mean it.

Some readers will probably be a bit sceptical about this. Fair enough – it's up to you what you experiment with. But you could start with an affirmation: 'I, ——, am open-minded and prepared to give this method a try!'

SECURITY, FAITH AND HOPE

You cannot manage yourself if you see and experience your life as being a random set of events, at the mercy of whatever buffeting forces happen to come along. You need to have a reasonable sense of *faith*, *security* and *hope*.

Let's look at what we mean by these terms. You could say that they relate to the way you *now* (i.e. in the present) feel about the past and the future. Has your past left you feeling reasonably secure, in yourself, your relationships, your job? Or, as a result of things that have happened to you, do you have a general feeling of insecurity, of isolation, of being different from others, since they seem to be able to cope much better, or their lives appear much kinder to them?

Similarly, when peering into the future can you see the shadow of some horrible, frightening uncertainty looming? Or are you able to look forward with confidence, with a faith that, within reason, no matter what comes along you have resources either within you or around you to cope or, better still, manage the situation?

Ideally, then, to manage ourselves really effectively we need *security* (based largely on past experiences), with *faith* now that we can look forward with *hope* to the future.

Most of us, though, are somewhere between these two extremes; that is, we have some degree of security, faith and hope, but perhaps not as much as we would like. Or, perhaps, it may be that the way you feel varies from time to time, according to your mood and/or depending on circumstances.

You can get a much better picture of the way you feel by some of the methods described elsewhere in this book. For example, the daily backwards review method (Chapter 3) can show which situations, people, events affect your feelings of security, faith and hope – and the subsequent effect on you and on others around you that those feelings in turn have.

Similarly, you can use analysis of critical incidents, or repertory grids (again, both described in Chapter 3) for the same purpose.

And it may be that once you understand what is happening and why, you will then be able to summon up your higher self, as discussed earlier in this chapter, to tame your insecurities, to take hope, to have faith; perhaps some of your unhelpful feelings are the result of the 'irrational assumptions' we looked at earlier? Perhaps some appropriate affirmations will help? And remember, there are four ways of moving on constructively: changing the situation, leaving it, changing yourself, or coming to terms with it.

However you choose to tackle this one, there's no doubt that working with others – either as a pair or in a group (Chapter 7) – can be of enormous help when seeking to increase your security, faith or hope. The very process of listening to others, sharing your own concerns, getting things off your chest, discovering you are not the only one who . . ., discovering friends, allies, contacts and comrades, can be enormously strengthening in this respect.

If, despite these ways of working on your ups and downs, you still feel pretty low when it comes to hope, faith and security, then you might well find that a more macro-approach is helpful. For this purpose we suggest you consider biography work, which sets out to look at events and themes in the past, and how they are affecting you now, before moving on, with increased sense of meaning and purpose, to examine the life questions now facing you as you look to the future.

Like many of the activities in this book, you *can* work with your biography, in the way that we will now examine, on your own, although you are likely to get much more from the process by doing it together with somebody else, or, ideally, in a small group.

BIOGRAPHY WORK

We will describe here a structured way of working that enables you to get an overview of your life so far (i.e. the *past*), which, when connected to the questions coming your way now (the *present*) enable you to make purposeful decisions about the *future*. It is convenient to look on it as a seven-step process.

Step 1: **Events**. You may recall that in Chapter 3 we looked at something called 'backwards review', involving going over the day's events in reverse order. Well, this first stage in biography work is more or less the same, except that this time you are looking back over the whole of your life so far, identifying incidents that stand out.

So, what you do is start in the present and think back over your life. What are the main events, incidents or happenings that you can recall? Identify these and write them down. An incident/event, by the way, might be something that happened very quickly, that was pretty short in time, or it might have taken place over quite a long period, and yet still be recognizable to you as a specific happening.

When you have identified your events, going back as far as you want, take a piece of paper – the larger the better – and draw your 'life-map', as though the bottom edge of the paper is a time axis. What and how you draw in the events against time is up to you; the most common method is to make a sort of graph, or life-line, by plotting your general level of feelings about life (e.g. on some qualitative scale like 'dreadful – wonderful') and then marking in, on that line, the various events that you have identified, as in Figure 4.1. Quite a different way, however, is to construct a collage of your life, by using pictures, words, etc. cut from newspapers and magazines that in some way are illustrative, symbolic, indicative of your life at that time.

Whatever method (or methods) you choose or devise, if you are working with a partner, or in a group, now is the time to share and discuss your events together.

Step 2: **Periods**. You now have a picture or chart of some key events in your life. (We say 'some' because obviously you cannot possibly identify them all at any single attempt. Don't worry about this – just recall what you can. When the time is ready you will, if you have another go at the exercise, remember some other events as well.) The next step is to look at the spaces *between* these events, to see if you can give these descriptions. You can get an idea of this from Figure 4.1 again, but do remember that these are only examples; the important thing is to look at *your* life, and see if you can identify periods between *your* events. Again, you can share and discuss these with your partner(s).

Step 3: **Themes**. The next thing to do is to look over your events and periods and see what *themes* you can recognize or identify. What do we mean by 'theme'? Well, in general it might be:

- a recurring pattern – of thoughts, feelings, behaviour, occurrences
- a constant feature of you or your life – or a feature that is there from time to time
- a tendency for certain things to happen
- particular aspects of yourself – including both your higher and lower self (Chapter 3) – making themselves apparent

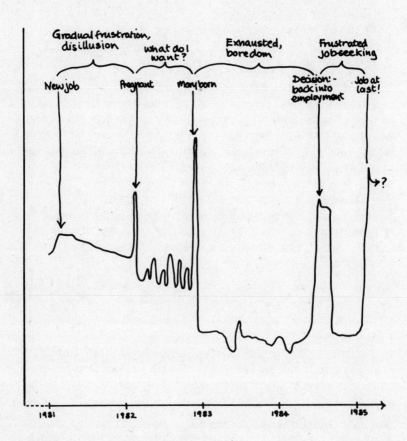

Figure 4.1

For example, some of the themes that we have seen in managers' biographies include:

- a tendency to undervalue myself
- recurring periods of ill-health
- travel abroad
- a pattern of problems when working with men
- conflict between my responsibilities as a mother and what seems to be expected of me at work
- a very strong tendency to put myself second – to give way to other people's needs and ignore my own
- fear of new and unknown situations
- close family ties
- a strong tendency to be so independent that I will never do anything that anyone else suggests I do
- the 'spoilt child' in me – the way I react when I don't get my own way
- initiating things, starting them off, for others to take up and complete

However, these are only indicative; it's *your* themes that are important. And here it can be extremely useful to work with others; they can give you feedback, ask you questions, and so on, about themes they think they might have spotted when you were sharing your events and periods.

At this point you might start to get some feelings – positive or negative – about some of the themes in your life. If so, contemplate these for a while, but don't yet get too involved in deciding what to do about them. This comes later in the overall process, in the next step.

Step 4: **Questions/issues coming my way**. As far as the biography process is concerned there are three main ways of highlighting life questions. Once again, working with others on their biographies can be especially useful here.

1 *The overall picture of your life.* Imagine that your biography is in fact that of someone else – he or she has

115

been describing it to you. What are your thoughts about that biography? What are your feelings? What do you see as that person's unfinished business? What do they need to be facing up to? What decisions or choices do they need to take? What is their biography saying to them? What are they achieving with their life? What remains to be achieved?

Then, remember that 'they' is you.

Note again that we are looking here for *questions* coming your way. You can concentrate more specifically on answers to those questions – in the form of intentions, plans and actions – later (see Chapter 2).

2 *Themes*. Very often we can get a good indication of questions that we need to be facing by considering our life themes. What do they seem to be telling you? What are your thoughts about them? Can you recognize any patterns among the themes – e.g.:

- have some themes disappeared from your life?
- have some only just appeared?
- do some come and go? If so, is there any pattern, or any set of causes, for this?

How do you feel about the themes, and/or the patterns amongst them? What are they saying to you, or asking you? Are they pointing to any decisions or choices that you need to make?

3 *People in your consciousness*. Your events, periods and themes will undoubtedly have involved a lot of other people. Some of these, no doubt, will be people with whom you have more or less frequent contact in your current everyday living. Others, however, may be physically much more distant. Indeed, you may not have seen them, or thought about them, for years. Others may indeed be dead; or not yet alive (e.g. a child you are currently carrying, or could never have). And yet, if they have emerged as a result of the previous steps in the biography process, they

are part of the network of people you carry around in your consciousness – even if, perhaps, until now you were hardly aware of that.

These members of your 'consciousness-net' may well be the source of questions for you. So as not to overload yourself, you may have to choose just a few to start with. Take each in turn. What are your thoughts, ideas, beliefs about that person? And about the fact that she is part of your consciousness-net? How do you feel about him? And his being in your consciousness? What is she saying to me? What questions, decisions or choices are coming my way through or because of him?

You might also like to think about people who do *not* seem to be in your consciousness. What is this telling you or asking you?

Steps 5, 6 and 7: **Intentions, resolutions and actions**. We have already looked at these in Chapter 2; so you can enter the prioritizing and decision-making process from this point.

5 Being skilful

Skills are the way we translate our awareness into action. Yet skill
– the ability to do something well as a result of practice – cannot be
defined without the awareness that makes it possible or without
the action that displays skilled performance:

> He sparks the torch, and sets a tiny little blue flame and then,
> it's hard to describe, actually dances the torch and the rod in
> separate little rhythms over the thin metal sheet, the whole spot
> a uniform luminous orange-yellow, dropping the torch and the
> filter-rod down at the exact moment and then removing them.
> No holes. You can hardly see the weld. 'That's beautiful' I say.
> 'One dollar' he says, without smiling . . . probably he thinks
> I'm bullshitting him. Who appreciates work like this anymore?
> (Robert M. Pirsig, *Zen and the Art of Motorcycle Maintenance*)

In this chapter we build upon the self-knowledge and awareness
which form the focus of Chapters 3 and 4 by providing a
framework for developing skills which will help you manage yourself more effectively.

WHAT ARE SKILLS?

Skills are learned qualities which belong to the individual. They do
not belong to trades, organizations or any other collectivity. Each
of us possesses some skills; they are part of us and can't be sensibly
described except as personal qualities. The skills we possess help
to define us and are part of our identity. Skills are satisfying to
acquire as long as they are within our range of possibilities and as

long as the environment in which we learn them is broadly supportive of that learning. Once learned, skills can be deeply satisfying to practise, however simple and mundane. Making pastry, writing a letter in italic script, digging, carrying out a recruitment interview, even sweeping, washing up and scrubbing floors, can be highly enjoyable performances (as long as you don't have to do them all and every day at someone else's command!). Doing these things well requires competence, good timing and an appropriate opportunity. Because skilled action displays control and confidence, few things are more healing and satisfying to us. Because most skills are by definition useful, they make a valuable contribution to the well-being of others. While I'm exercising a skill, for those five or ten minutes I'm in charge, mistress or master of my world. Beyond competence, the performance of a skill has a beauty of its own. A few years ago at the Winter Olympics the British skaters Torvill and Dean captured the hearts of the public with a supreme exhibition of skill upon the ice. Their control, timing and confidence were such that their performance transcended the normal criteria even of world-class skating to become an artistic act. Millions of people not normally hooked on skating were spellbound and touched in that special way which marks the mystical or spiritual experience. This skilled skating performance had the same effect upon us as great music, painting or poetry.

All skills can be practised at the level of art, where suddenly the effort disappears and the performance becomes effortless. When we're lucky enough to be performing at this level, as Torvill and Dean were that year, we literally feel that 'we can't put a foot wrong'. Here there is a sense of participation in something larger than our individual lives. Artists serve their material, allow it to pass through them, their long technical practice a necessary but insufficient component of the performance. It is enough to be the instrument, to have the opportunity of moving beyond the daily limitations of being inside ourselves. Not that the artistic performance can be summoned up entirely by our will, we can only prepare ourselves and put ourselves in the way for it. And we are not talking Great Art here. I remember playing darts at times

119

when I had a premonition of just where the dart would go, a mysterious connection between hand, eye, mind's eye and dartboard for that moment. As the Zen Buddhists say, the archer must cease to aim in order to hit the target. The footballer's 'magic' is a recognition of the same rare, but universally recognized, moment.

While most of us have this sort of experience in our lives somewhere, we don't have it every day, all the time. Most of the time we don't need this level of performance, and it is clear that when we describe something as skilful we're talking about different degrees or levels of skill. Indeed in the great heyday of craftsmanship, these levels of skill were formally recognized as statuses. You began as an apprentice, served your time and passed out to be a journeyman. Some people went on to become master craftsmen, and a very few attained the status of artists. (These statuses of a bygone age parallel our stages of managing in Table 3.2.)

The *apprentice*	is learning the rules, procedures and standard ways of doing things. The apprentice tries to do the 'right' thing, and copies elders and betters, spending most of the time practising. (Stage 1, Table 3.2.)
The *journeyman*	is one who operates on the norms and conventions of the trade and who can do the job in an acceptable and competent way. The journeyman can do most jobs in accordance with current standards. (Stage 2, Table 3.2.)
The *master*	is beyond simple competence and is able to apply skill in new and complex situations. Flexibility and creativity are important; the master tackles the non-standard jobs. (Stage 3, Table 3.2.)
The *artist*	is a master craftsperson who operates with a wider awareness in diverse and trackless conditions with a clear sense of purpose. Able to

contribute to the particular needs of the time, the artist serves a higher purpose than just doing a job. (Stages 4 and 5, Table 3.2.)

While few of us are going to reach the Torvill and Dean status, we can achieve artistic levels in what we do, given the right combination of abilities, circumstances and motivation. Of course, most of what we do doesn't require skill at this level – I'm quite happy as a journeyman gardener and an apprentice poultry-keeper, although I'm pleased that I've mastered cooking and on occasions achieve truly artistic effects.

This is a coming together of necessity and motivation – I have the basic abilities for learning to cook (most of us do); there are circumstances requiring me to cook and encouraging me to do so; and I'm motivated to do better in cooking than in, say, gardening or poultry-keeping, and much more so than in, say, rabbit-shooting, which I positively don't want to do. I try harder at cooking, get feedback from a (usually) appreciative bunch of consumers and derive much satisfaction from it. In my house I'm quite a famous cook – one of the most famous, in fact! Doing a job that needs doing, having a chance to practise my art; all this and fame too – what more can I ask from life? (Well, quite a lot, actually, but it's a start.)

HOW SKILFUL ARE YOU?

Let's now take a look at your skills and how well you do them. Why have you learned some skills and not others? Why have you continued learning in some and put others on automatic? Table 5.1 lists some general life skills together with a grading system across the top to check whether you have the skill at all and, if so, at what level. Of course this is only a selection of everyday skills; many are missing, and we've left a few lines at the bottom for you to put in some of yours which may be left out.

Table 5.1 Skills with things

Skill	Level of skill				
	Can't/ don't do	Apprentice	Competent worker	Craftsperson	Artist
1 Cooking					
2 Painting and decorating					
3 Woodwork					
4 Sewing					
5 Knitting					
6 Gardening					
7 Playing a musical instrument					
8 Typing/ keyboard skills					
9 Handwriting					
10 Electrical work					
11 Clothes- making					
12 Driving					
13 Car main- tenance					
14 Operating CCTV/video equipment					
15 Plumbing					
16 Household budgeting					
17 Ironing					
18					
19					
20					

etc.

There are all sorts of reasons why you have or have not learned some of these skills. One of the most interesting columns in your table will be the first. Look at the pattern it reveals in terms of those things you can't or don't do. What does this say about you and your attitude to skills? One of the criticisms of much formal management training is that it is too concerned with what we might call 'rational skills' – teaching everyone techniques for problem-solving, decision-making, time-management, selling and so on as if we all had the same problems or were not practising these skills because we don't know how to. Apart from the fact that life isn't all that rational, there are uniquely personal patterns to our skills development and to the skills we will have learned so far in life which determine to a large extent which new skills we will learn and to what standard. To take an obvious example, if I've never learned to type because I see myself as not very dextrous, or because I'm 'useless with machines' or because I expect others to do the menial work, then I'm less likely to want to tackle the operation of a word processor or a computer, or perhaps to operate CCTV or any sort of machine. On the other hand, if I'm good with machines or 'handy' then I might well pick up these skills in preference to others, say, involving communicating with other people.

Looking down your left-hand column, let's consider the possible reasons why you've not learned some of these very useful life skills.

Somewhere along the line between birth and adulthood we make decisions which determine that we'll learn some skills and not others. The young child wants to learn everything and is very eager to tackle all new skills – crawling, walking, talking, reading – unless actively discouraged. This eagerness to learn can be a problem; leave scissors within reach of a two-year-old and she'll try to learn how to use them. By the time we're adolescent, however, we start asserting ourselves, defining ourselves by what we pay attention to and learn, and what we won't or don't. Can I get my kids to garden? Cook? Paint the front door? Well, perhaps, but often not. Maybe they'll learn some of these things later, perhaps not. As adolescents we start deciding for ourselves *not* to learn certain skills, and also, perhaps, to concentrate upon others. This is part of realizing our autonomy but it has implications for how we will tackle the skills of managing ourselves and others later in life.

So, as adults, what determines why we learn some skills and not others? Why is it that you can't boil an egg or drive a car at your age?

In no particular order, here are some reasons which, if they apply to you, will be continuing to apply to you in the job that you do and how you manage. First, our skills are part of our identity and, as we saw in Chapter 4, what we manage to do or stop ourselves doing depends upon how we see ourselves. In general our fear of failure stops us tackling things which we feel are beyond us. As sisters or brothers we might avoid or respond to rivalry, determined not to learn to knit because 'she does it', or wanting to learn to cook because 'big brother does it'. The pattern of what we'll learn or not is usually to do with being independent/dependent. Obviously we learn to drive, cook, budget in order to be independent and live our own lives, but why do we *not* learn to cook, sew, drive, type, budget? Could it be that we expect mummy or daddy (or mummy and daddy's replacements) to do these things for us? A male friend has learned to cook a proper Sunday dinner after much battling and struggle, internal and external, and can do everything very well except make the gravy. At gravy time he calls down the original cook and gets her to make it. Does he really not know how and is unable to learn to make gravy? It's hard to believe, isn't it? Especially as elsewhere he can dismantle and reassemble jukeboxes and pinball machines. No, he doesn't make the gravy because that is his sticking point beyond which he is not prepared to be independent. He wants to remain dependent in this; maybe he wants to make the point at each meal that this is her proper job really, or perhaps to get her to notice how well he's done. Didn't he do well!

Have you discovered any of your dependency patterns yet? Now let's look at the rest of the table. Are you a multi-skilled person or a specialist? Are you one of life's craftspersons in everything you do, or have you a good spread – learning or apprenticed in some things, an artist in others? Do you settle for competence in all things, never letting your reach exceed your grasp, or do you strive continuously for perfection, artistry, even in sweeping the hall? The pattern you can see here in these life skills, mainly with things, learned in childhood and adolescence to a large extent, will probably mirror the pattern with more complex social and managing skills. Can you see your pattern?

THE SKILLS OF MANAGING

Generally speaking there are three broad groupings of useful skills:

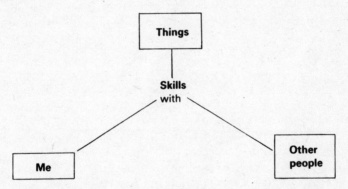

We have talked about skills with *things* although there are some more complex 'things' in managing – plans, accounts, budgets, forecasts, policies and so on – which most managers need at least some competence in. You will probably find that your patterns and preferences as revealed by Table 5.1 apply as much to these more complex 'things' of managing as they do to the more mundane and basic life skills. Much of this book is about skills with ME – managing yourself. In particular, Chapters 2, 3 and 4 are aimed at helping you become more aware of your strengths and weaknesses and how you can manage yourself with regard to your awareness, perception, self-love and self-hate, self-control and imagination and intuition. In addition there are some very practical skills with yourself such as managing your time, diary management, developing good working habits and so on. Some of these are discussed in detail by other books in this series, such as Sally Garratt's *Manage Your Time*. As we've said above, much of management training and development has concentrated, not surprisingly, upon these rational, practical skills, so that there are resources around should you wish to pursue these avenues. Some of the skills which are particularly crucial to good managing are those used in dealings with *other people*.

Here is another table, in which you can mark your level of skill with *other people*. Don't be falsely modest. Try for a spread of skill levels and avoid the safety of ticking down the middle.

Table 5.2 Skills with other people

Skill	Level of skill				
	Can't/ won't do	Apprentice	Competent worker	Crafts- person	Artist
1 Interviewing					
2 Speaking in public					
3 Selling things					
4 Striking up a conversation					
5 Serving on a committee					
6 Talking about myself/ expressing feelings openly					
7 Saying what I want					
8 Saying 'No'					
9 Encouraging others and building them up					
10 Working as a team/group member					
11 Speaking on the telephone					
12 Complaining in a shop/ restaurant					
13 Giving others 'bad' news					
14 Giving others 'good' news					
15 Speaking up when I think something is wrong					
16 Relating as an equal to authority, e.g. police, teachers					
17 Relating as an equal to 'subordinates', e.g. cleaners, clerical, canteen staff					
18					
19					
etc.					

Skills with *other people* are quite crucial to managing. While skills with *things*, and in particular your pattern of learning these, will tell you much about your propensity and ability to learn certain skills in certain situations, it is these skills with *other people* which are likely to mark out good managing. So it is worth going through your pattern on this table to see how it has been formed.

Start with those skills you haven't learned or don't want to learn. Why is this? Is it to do with 'sibling rivalry'? Fear of failure probably comes into it quite a lot, and so will those patterns of independence and dependence. You will have had some of these skills from an early age, possessing natural ability perhaps. There will probably be a heavy influence of conditioning from your parents and others. Were you told, 'Children should be seen but not heard'? Or were you encouraged to join in? Little girls are often encouraged to say 'Yes' rather than 'No' and to do what others want rather than follow their own desires. Many resist this sort of conditioning, even developing strong skills in opposition to this sort of pressure. Little boys are encouraged sometimes to be forward, to fend for themselves and to take initiatives with other people. Sometimes this encourages us to develop these skills and sometimes quite the opposite. If you did the contrary to what your teachers and parents wanted, then you've still been just as much formed by that conditioning.

It is important to understand the pattern of which skills you've learned and which you haven't, and why, before you go forward. If you don't understand these early influences and patterns, then you may try to work against rather than with them.

The starting point, then, is – what skills with *yourself*, with *things* and with *other people* do you want to develop? What do you *not* want to work on?

THE SKILLS DEVELOPMENT PROCESS

How do you go about developing a skill? What is the process involved? Let's illustrate this with an example from your own experience:

128

Think of a skill you've learned at some point in the past. Any skill will do – perhaps one from the two tables in this chapter.

Think back to the time when you *didn't* have this skill. What was life like then? How did you feel about yourself? Who did you know who did have this skill? How did you see them in relation to yourself?

Now, what made you *choose* to learn this skill? Where did your motivation or incentive come from?

Next, think back to how you recognized what this skill meant in practice. How did you get a *picture* of what skilled performance was? Did you have a model or models to help you get the idea? Perhaps colleagues or members of your family served as examples of competent workers or craftspersons in this particular skill?

What *target* or goal did you set yourself? How did you fix this?

Now think about the *practising* you did. Do you remember how long it took? How did you feel when you had to practise? Was it enjoyable, tedious, hard work?

What do you remember about getting *feedback* about your performance? Who told you how you were doing, how you were getting on? Did you feel supported and encouraged by other people when you were trying to learn the skill or not? What effect did this have?

Working through your own personal case example will have demonstrated the characteristics of the skills development process. People learn things in different ways, but most will share these seven elements:

1 Choosing the skill to be learned
2 Choosing the level or target to aim at
3 Finding a model or models to imitate

4 Observing the skilled performance of your model(s)
5 Having opportunities to practise
6 Obtaining feedback on your performance
7 Being supported in learning

This last one is more important to us than we might at first think. To acknowledge the need for learning demands real courage for the adult manager – we're supposed to be self-sufficient, complete already. We need support to believe that learning new skills is a healthy, natural process of renewal; that it is in fact the norm and not the other way round. Getting started on learning a new skill involves a lot of choosing. This means managing ME and taking personal responsibility for making the commitment of time and attention. We all learn a lot from modelling – sitting next to Nelly or Norman and watching them do it. How much of your managing have you learned this way? More than you care to admit? Perhaps more than is good for you because managing yourself first and then others is something intensely personal. Although we can learn a lot from others, we need plenty of practice and feedback to help us learn our own way of doing things. Feedback and then the support you need to keep going, especially when stuck on the arid plateau of the learning curve, illustrate once again that you can't go very far in managing yourself without help from other people. This is perhaps the central paradox of self-managing – that as soon as you take personal responsibility for your health, skills and so on, you really need the ideas, feedback resources and support of others. You can't manage alone. In Chapter 7 there are various ideas for ways of enlisting the help and support of other people in your-self-managing efforts.

Let's now work back through the skills development process with a skill which you would like to learn, either from scratch or to a higher degree of proficiency:

Choose a skill from one of the two tables in this chapter, or pick one of your own which is relevant to managing yourself or other people. Select one that you really do want to learn, perhaps one that you've never had time – or given time – to, or one that you've learned some first steps in, perhaps many years ago, and that you'd like to take further.

Now *visualize* what it would be like to have this skill. What would you be doing with it? Where would you be doing it? Who with? How would you feel if you were practising this skill?

Think about your *motivation* for learning this skill. How strong is this? What level of effort will it support? How can you build up your commitment?

Given your level of motivation, what do you think would be a realistic *target* to attain by the end of this week? By the end of this month? In three months' time? Again, visualize these targets – get a picture of what you could do at the end of the week, month etc. Set a series of realistic goals.

How much time and opportunity have you for *practice*? How much practice will be necessary for you to achieve these targets? Make out a practice timetable and book these practice slots in your diary.

Perhaps you can't decide on targets and practice time until you've found a *model*. Who do you know who is willing to serve as a model for you to learn from? If you can find more than one then that's better still.

Ask your models for *feedback* about your practice efforts. Whatever the skill you're practising, you need people who can observe you in action to give you some feedback. You can also provide it for yourself by reviewing your practice immediately afterwards, going through what happened step by step and looking for improvements you can make.

Finally, what sources of *support* can you draw on? Who will encourage you, nag you to practise, remind you of your resolve, think about you and talk to you? Recruiting a 'speaking partner' or building up your network of support is an important part of the process.

Embarking on the development of a skill is like any other subject – it needs managing. You can manage skills development all the better for visualizing the process and investing some time in planning.

'MASTERY' TO MYSTERY

The last great threshold in skills development lies beyond 'mastery'. When we think of ourselves learning a skill, we see ourselves as becoming more and more competent, our control and timing better and better. Yet for many of the skills involved in managing ME and other people, the notion of perfect competence is illusory. In human affairs, those who deal with us in a 'practised' way – the doctor's 'bedside manner'; the teacher's elegant explanation – attract both admiration and irritation. We feel reassured by the professionalism yet patronized by what is ultimately stereotypical treatment. We are not a thing to be worked on to perfection! In our contrary way we demand both competence and professionalism *and* spontaneity and creativity in human interaction. Everyone gets it wrong sometimes – infallibility in human affairs would be deeply disturbing, and which of us is so competent that we are sufficient, complete in a way which admits no need for further learning?

So here lies another paradox – the progression from learner to competent worker to craftsperson to artist is not a gradient of gradually increasing competence, edging step by step to perfection. There is a threshold where 'mastery' must give way to mystery, where the creativity of the artist demands the need to get it wrong and to strive against 'impossible' standards. The standards of artistry are not attainable on a regular basis of competence. We recognize this possibility in almost all skills. If a person were to describe themselves as 'perfect' at managing we should rightly think them, if not deranged, then certainly as appallingly complacent. Beyond a certain level of competence we can only continue to improve if we allow ourselves to admit into ourselves the mysteriousness of things. The manager as artist is marked by a determination to give up 'mastery' and transform it into mystery by becoming aware of the fullness and infinite variety of things. To put it another way, as soon as we can accomplish something well, we become ready to take the next step, to tackle the next problem which is, at this moment, mysterious. Development enables us to tackle the next problem, the next mystery. Going beyond competence into mystery requires the use of all our powers of sensing. Rudolf Steiner's work suggests that there are a number of 'super senses' beyond our normally accepted view of the five senses – touch, taste, hearing, smell and sight. As our senses are the primary ways in which we learn and develop our skills, this is a proposition of immense significance.

For example, we have all experienced occasions when we somehow just *know* what to say, *when* to speak, *who* to look at, or whatever. We sometimes say that this is a 'sixth sense' or 'it was nothing, just common sense'. In fact this is anything but 'common' sense, it's just that we find it difficult to be aware of how/why/what we did, when we did. It's all a bit mysterious. What we can say is that in these situations we behaved very skilfully but we don't know quite how. Usually these situations are not to do with things, but involve skills either with oneself or with other people.

The 'super' senses

In Figure 5.1 with me at the centre, I develop most of my skills with myself, with things and with other people through the medium of the normal 'five senses'. Artistry demands we get in touch with the super senses which lie beyond. Only through these can we take our skills beyond competence:

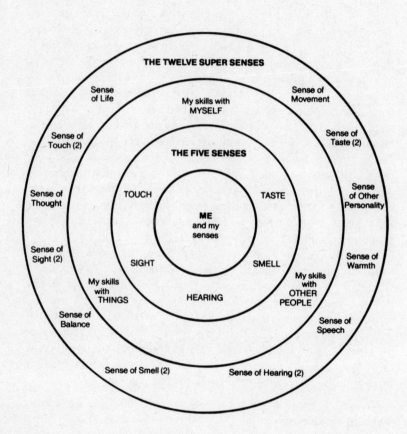

Briefly these twelve super senses are as follows:

1 Sense of life An awareness of your state of well-being, physical self, aliveness, mood etc. 'How are you feeling today?' we say. This awareness of life enables you to take into account the effect of your mood upon others and theirs upon you.

2 Sense of movement At the physical level this tells you whether you're moving or standing still, and makes you aware of the relative movements of parts of your body. For example, it is this sense that enables you to touch the end of your nose with your eyes shut. At a deeper level this is a sense which tells you when it's time to make a move, to do or to say something. We say, 'I felt moved to . . . (action).'

3 Sense of balance At the physical level it's what enables you to stand up without falling over. At a deeper level, we may say someone is unbalanced or knocked off balance. We are aware of this sense when we describe ourselves or others as well-balanced, grounded or steady.

4 Sense of warmth We talk of getting warmed up for doing something or of feeling warm towards someone. We describe others as warm or cold and we can sense when we are getting warm – getting to the heart of things.

5 Sense of speech When we listen we hear more than the noise a person makes – we say, 'I'm getting the sense of what you're saying', being an understanding of what the other person is thinking, feeling and willing. We hear the music as well as the words – what's said, what's not said, we note the phrasing and similies, intonations, gestures, facial expressions etc.

6 Sense of thought As when we say, without the other person speaking, 'I know what you're thinking.' The fully developed sense of thought would be telepathy.

7 Sense of other personality Although first impressions can be wrong, we often get a sense, within a few minutes of meeting them, of what makes another person as they are. A blind French Resistance leader in the Second World War developed this super sense of personality to such a degree that he was able to judge whether or not candidates who presented themselves for the Resistance could be trusted or not. All those he rejected turned out to be spies. On one occasion his colleagues overruled him because the candidate had such good credentials. A few days later they were all betrayed by this man whom the blind leader had correctly sensed to be a danger.

The last five super senses are the transformed versions of the normal five senses:

8 Sense of sight A sense of vision or foresight as in 'I see what you mean' or 'I can see difficulties ahead'. Sometimes we may refer to 'second sight' in those who can foresee coming events.

9 Sense of touch Being in touch with the situation and with other people; having a feel for what's happening or what someone is doing.

10 Sense of hearing As in 'Does that ring bells for you?' or 'I'm getting strong vibrations from her'. We talk of things resonating within us.

11 Sense of taste As when we notice a pleasant or unpleasant taste to something – 'That leaves a nasty taste in the mouth' or 'This is just to my taste'.

12 Sense of smell We frequently sniff out situations and perhaps smell 'a rat' or feel that 'something smells fishy'. We say that we can detect 'a whiff of conspiracy in the air'.

These are Rudolf Steiner's twelve super senses through which we can develop mystery – become intuitive and convert craft into art. But how can we learn to acquire these hidden, higher senses? Regularly carrying out activities such as 'backwards review' (Chapter 2) and 'being aware of what's going on inside you' – your own thinking, feeling, willing (Chapter 2) – do help to develop these 'sixth' senses. Creative visualization and making affirmations, creating silence and space for listening to your inner self through meditating (Chapter 6), will all contribute to this goal which is sometimes described as the opening of the 'Third Eye' or of the 'inner sense organs'.

Perhaps you are finding this discussion far-fetched or at least somewhat strange? Well, that's quite right – it is strange, not to say weird. But how would you expect the mysterious to look? Some of these ideas are already being used, for example in medicine to open up the sense of life – health = whole = well balanced – and meditation, creative visualization and other ideas are being increasingly used with cancer patients and others who suffer from 'stress diseases'. These senses are not 'normal', mad people and artists may have known them, but they remain largely hidden to us who live in the world of the five senses. Blind people and others who are handicapped are more likely to have learned some of these super skills to compensate for their lack of 'normal' senses. However, if we wish to go beyond 'mastery' in managing ourselves and others, we have to search in these mysterious depths.

6 Managing your health

The 36-year-old managing director of a supermarket chain was found dead in his car. He had driven out into the country and connected a tube from the exhaust pipe into the car. Later it was found that he had been sacked from his job just ten hours previously. His former Chairman was quoted as saying three things . . . 'We are all deeply shocked' . . . 'Although he was very competent at sales and marketing, he unfortunately neglected the day-to-day running of the company' . . . and . . . 'He was an extremely tough character and he took the news like a man.'

This true and horrific incident happened in England in 1980. It is a dramatic example of some of the effects of managerial work. We can only guess at the turmoil and pain which led this poor man to take this way out. We can get some clues from the Chairman about his work environment. Clearly a highly successful man, in a top job at a young age, making an important contribution, is suddenly and brutally removed from office. Acknowledged to be good at some things, he is judged to be bad at others. He took the news 'like a man', preserved his tough image to the end without a tremor or a tear or a plea for understanding and help. The cost of this was insupportable and this man could not bear it. At some times and in some cultures this is a route for heroes – the British Captain Oates walking into the Arctic cold so as not to burden his companions; the Japanese Samurai disembowelling himself rather than face dishonour – and sometimes the managerial culture reflects these echoes.

HOW WELL ARE YOU MANAGING YOUR HEALTH?

These are dramatic comparisons compared with most managerial work. Yet the working lives of managers and professionals are often demanding as well as sedentary. We sometimes work long hours that spill over into weekends and evenings; we may end up drinking and eating too much at working meals; we are responsible for others in circumstances where expediency and moral values clash; we sometimes pursue careers single-mindedly, uprooting our families frequently to climb the ladder; we may commute long distances and endure tiring business trips; we pressure ourselves with demands for greater excellence or higher achievement and so on. We work under pressure, to deadlines and often from chairs behind desks. Stress and pressure cause a number of physiological responses in human beings, for example:

- increased rate of breathing
- increased production of adrenalin and other hormones
- increased secretion of cholesterol in the liver
- constriction of blood vessels in key muscle areas
- faster heart beat to increase blood supply

all of which help prepare us for action; physical action. These are instinctive responses triggered by the autonomous nervous system, without which we'd never have survived the Stone Age. When faced with danger or threat, we have a number of choices, the most obvious of which are perhaps *flight* or *fight*.

Our Stone Age forebears needed these instinctive physical changes and responses to cope with predators and used this physical arousedness in real flight or fight. The monsters we meet in managerial work are a bit different – frustrating meetings, people who let us down, unfair criticisms, failing to meet targets and deadlines, having to do things we don't like or approve of. Nonetheless, monsters they are, and instinctively, if not consciously, our bodies recognize this.

139

BEHAVIOUR AT WORK QUIZ

How do you cope with these monsters? Are you easily irritated and frustrated, do you feel intolerant a lot of the time? Or are you mostly quite relaxed at work, tolerant, easy-going, taking it all in your stride? Here's a little quiz on your behaviour at work. Ring the number on each scale that best characterizes your *usual* response or behaviour, i.e. 1 or 5 if you are *very* like the behaviour described at either end; 2 or 4 if you *lean* towards this one or that; and 3 if you're genuinely in balance between the two poles.

Are you/do you:

1 Casual about timekeeping	1 2 3 4 5	Punctual, never late
2 Do things at easy pace	1 2 3 4 5	Do things quickly (eat, walk, move etc.)
3 Never rushed, even under pressure	1 2 3 4 5	Always rushing about
4 Take time out to think and relax	1 2 3 4 5	Never stop to think; feel guilty about relaxing at work
5 Do one thing at a time	1 2 3 4 5	Keep several 'balls in the air' at once
6 Uncompetitive, avoid conflict	1 2 3 4 5	Very competitive, relish combat

7 Feel as though   1 2 3 4 5   Always feel a
there's plenty   sense of urgency
of time

8 Have many   1 2 3 4 5   Mainly interested
interests; talk   in work; talk a lot
about many   about work
topics

Now add up all the ringed numbers for your total ———

Before interpreting your score, let's examine the theory behind the quiz. Since the early 1970s, some of the work on occupational stress has focused upon the link between personality and the tendency to get highly stressed or not. Friedman and Rosenman, two heart specialists from San Francisco, are responsible for suggesting that there is a relationship between coronary heart disease and certain types of behaviour. Their 'Type A' person exhibits the following:

- extreme competitiveness
- continuous striving for achievement
- aggressiveness
- impatience and restlessness
- hyperalertness
- explosiveness of speech
- tenseness of facial musculature
- feelings of being under pressure all the time
- feels a chronic sense of urgency, of struggle

Their 'Type B' person, on the other hand, exhibits:

- little sense of time urgency
- harbours little 'free-floating aggression'
- feels little need to discuss or display achievements

141

- relaxes and plays without guilt
- slower and more easy-going in movement and speech
- less easily irritated, frustrated and angered

Friedman and Rosenman, followed by several other researchers since, are generally agreed that Type A people suffer more heart disease – between two and six times as much, depending upon the study.

Now, while checking your score, remember two other important things: first, that Friedman and Rosenman's Types A and B are 'ideal types', that is to say, composites of behaviour traits constructed to fit a theory. They are not real people, and no individual is actually like A or B. Secondly, managers who were close to Type B might have trouble getting by with all that lack of urgency and low needs for achievement, mightn't they? We might hypothesize that managerial work requires and attracts Type As. Many managers tend towards Type A because these are the 'pushers and movers', the people who fix things and get things done. Type As enjoy influencing their environment and making things happen, but they have associated problems. Those of us who lean towards Type A frequently overdo it – driving as if our lives depended upon shaving two seconds off the journey time; being unable to wait patiently in the shortest queue; using high energy on trivial tasks. In short we can become 'adrenalin freaks'; a pain to those around us – always pushing, aggressive, unsettling, never still; and a pain to ourselves, for the link between this type of behaviour and proneness to heart disease has been well demonstrated.

By now you Type As must be chewing the book in frustration waiting for the scoring! Beyond the joke, if you have noticed yourself getting a little irritated by the gap between the quiz and the scoring key, that is something to log and add to your diagnosis. If you scored:

between 8   and 15 – you are Type B (are you sure you're reading the right book?)
between 16   and 23 – you lean towards Type B

exactly 24   – Congratulations! or Cheat!
between 25 and 32 – you lean towards Type A
between 33 and 40 – you score 'A+'

If you lean towards Type B, your needs as a person and manager may well be more related to other chapters in this book, especially those on *Skills* and *Action*. If you tend towards Type A then you should pay even more attention to this chapter. Those characteristics that are serving you well in your managerial career may also be having some undesirable consequences. If so, you need to be continuously aware of health, in all its aspects – monitoring it regularly, diagnosing it from time to time and acting on it all the time.

One of the main problems is that we get physiologically aroused by all the stressors at work and there is no appropriate physical expression of all that preparedness – all that readiness for fighting and flighting – as there was for our Stone Age ancestors. Being subject to these stressors over long periods without appropriate release and expression is damaging to our health. The main killers of managers and professional workers between thirty-five and sixty-four are heart disease (easily the biggest), cancer and strokes. Heart disease killed a quarter of a million people in England alone in 1981, and over one million in the USA. These rates are rising.

However, the good news is that the risk of all these diseases can be reduced by developing healthy habits. The link between stress and heart disease and strokes is well known, and it is now becoming clear that a number of forms of cancer are related to the way we handle our emotions – to say nothing of those that are self-induced by smoking. We'll return to this later in this chapter.

Good health is not just about avoiding an early grave. Many stress-related illnesses are not killers – arthritis, asthma, ulcers, colitis, diabetes, eczema and migraines are just a few off this unpleasant list. Some of these illnesses may be psychosomatic, that is, physical manifestation of psychological disturbances. Beyond physical illness, good health means freedom from, or control over, *emotional* and *mental* distress. Emotional ills such as anxiety, fear, panic, anger, hatred, resentment and guilt, feelings of helplessness and inadequacy, can be as crippling as any physical illness. Mental distress such as hypertension, neurosis, manic depression, obsession, phobias and hysteria provide another field of disturbing possibilities.

Dividing these dangers to health into physical, emotional and mental has some benefits, although in other ways it is too simplistic – illnesses are things we have wrong with us as whole persons – body, soul and spirit. Nevertheless we use the distinction to talk about what you can do in various ways to guard against these dangers to survival and maintain yourself in good health. Before we go on to look at these three aspects of our health there are some very important attitudes to health which need examining. We'll start this off with another short quiz.

MY DESTRUCTIVE HABITS QUIZ

Here is a list of habits which are actually or potentially damaging to your health. Because each of us can control these habits, continuing with them is self-destructive. How much self-destruction do you indulge in?

Put a tick in the appropriate column for each item	I do this regularly	I do this sometimes	I never do this
1 Overeating – eating past the point of feeling well			
2 Eating the 'wrong' things – whatever they are			
3 Smoking			
4 Drinking more than is safe or necessary			
5 Using lifts instead of climbing stairs			
6 Driving distances of less than half a mile			
7 Not wearing your car seat belt when driving			
8 Bottling up anger, pain, grief and not telling anyone about it			
9 Harbouring suspicions, fears, anxieties and not checking them out			
10 Never giving yourself a break from work, duty, responsibilities			
11 etc. (Fill in here your own particular self-destructive habits.)			

There's no numerical scoring for this quiz, but take a look at the three columns. How many ticks do you have in Column 1? Column 2? Column 3? Remember that this is by no means a complete list – we human beings show a typical inventiveness in the things we can do to ourselves – and you should be able to add at least a couple of your own particular self-destructive habits.

We get into these habits for all sorts of reasons – through aping parents or other 'role models' years ago, at times of stress and so on – and they become habits because we no longer are aware of them; we don't stop to think about them or their potential effects. Some are a product of a 'First World lifestyle' where our high material standard of living in the 'First World' provides us with an abundance of food, alcohol, cigarettes, drugs, cars etc. Our health problems of heart disease, alcoholism, lung cancer, diabetes, obesity etc. reflect this lifestyle and are diseases of affluence. 'Third World' peoples are largely free from these diseases; they suffer instead from diseases of poverty – malnutrition, infections, epidemics – through lack of food, clean water, adequate housing and sanitation.

Managing your health is a critical aspect of 'self-development'. Pigging yourself at business lunches or bottling up feelings for fear of appearing weak doesn't do you any good at all and is a very bad example to others, encouraging them to be self-destructive too. It's bad for you, bad for them, bad for business.

So what can be done? Talk is cheap, and these habits are usually hard to break. The first step is to become aware of what you are doing. A protective habit we all share is the tendency to block our awareness of unpleasant facts; to wipe from the memory past actions, thoughts or sights which disturb us. We do the same thing with our bad habits. Part of us, of course – our higher self (Chapter 4) – knows how bad they are for us, but another part of us – our inner enemy – suppresses this truth.

In fact, allowing yourself to become simply aware is not at all simple. You're fighting your own 'self-protective' blanking out responses in becoming and remaining aware. Simple awareness, receptivity to what is happening can be painful. As someone said, human beings can only bear so much reality; but it is the key to tackling these habits and replacing them with healthy ones. A part of you – your inner friend – has always to remain on watch when you're in the pub, the restaurant, the office. Awareness and vigilance are the main actions required for the tough and lonely work of habit-breaking. Many people find it easier with the support of sympathetic allies, and women in particular have pioneered the use of support groups to help improve health and fitness. Enlisting the support of others is the second key step to healthy habits, especially because, if people aren't with you then they're probably against you. Those who press upon others extra drinks and 'just one' cigarette are looking for allies too – allies in self-destruction! In managerial work most of us are surrounded with such 'friends', and if you want to break your self-destructive habits and build new, healthy ones, then a support group or self-development group (see especially Chapter 7) could be part of the answer for you.

Stress and bad habits can lead to health problems. Sometimes we tend to think of stress-related illnesses as a managerial or executive problem. This is not the case at all – manual, clerical, technical and professional workers are as likely to suffer from stress as managerial workers. Poor conditions, monotonous work, overloading, tight targets, high quality standards, close supervision and many other aspects of work organization are potential stressors. Managers are lucky in that they usually have more discretion and more control over how they spend their working lives – or at least they should have! Yet of course it is this very characteristic of managerial work that brings the stress – conditions that also create the opportunities for individual initiatives and risk-taking that many of us thrive upon.

In discussing health we may tend to dwell too much on the debilitating effects of work, underemphasizing how exciting and fulfilling work is for many of us at times. We spend a large amount of our lives at work – those of us lucky enough to have jobs. We see it as good fortune to be in work because work provides so much for us, including money. Much of our social standing and status stems from the job. Work provides us with a time structure, by the day, week, year, and even for life. But work also allows us to feel competent in exercising skills and abilities in a collaborative production of useful goods or services. Moreover, much of our social lives and interactions with others, their ideas and beliefs, is found at work.

With all this and money too, it is no wonder that we count ourselves lucky to be 'in work'. No wonder that we recognize the modern affliction of 'workaholism' – of addiction to work; no wonder that some managers 'run on adrenalin' – it's legal, socially encouraged, it's good for business and it's even patriotic! Many of us get a real 'kick' out of our work – what would we turn to without it? Yet sometimes this habit 'work' becomes compulsive, taking over lives, blotting out family, leisure, friends, let alone politics, world affairs, music, art, games and all the other available riches. Retirement or redundancy loom ahead like wastelands – we try not to think of them.

While on this theme, let's remember that 'great work', as in the lives of poets, musicians, artists of all kinds, is often bad for your health. Many great artists die young. If the exhaustion induced in body, soul and spirit by producing great efforts doesn't kill us, then the frustration caused by the vision of great potential and the inability to attain it will drive us to drink, drugs and self-destruction. Few of us are great poets, but all of us are, in our own way, human artists. We set personal standards in our lives that we'd like to reach, and from time to time we dare to see if we can go that little bit farther. All of us, at some time or another, have felt the pull of that siren song urging us to greater efforts whatever the costs. At this point, we literally don't care about ourselves, the work is all, even at the cost of our self-sacrifice.

Each of us must make our own choice here – who is to say whether it would have been better for Franz Schubert to go a little easier upon himself, maybe even finish off his symphony, live to a ripe old age, instead of producing over six hundred incomparable songs and numerous other works in a short but phenomenally energetic burst, dying at thirty-one with a solid place in the history

If you did just this one exercise every day, the benefits to your health could be considerable. Tests on American managers showed that fifty steps a day significantly lowered susceptibility to heart disease. If you don't manage to do anything else in this book, do this. You could even then throw it away if you wish because you'd have had your money's worth and more!

A SIMPLE EXERCISE ROUTINE

Here's a bending and stretching exercise to start. Again, anyone can do this at their own speed and level of effort. The main thing to try and achieve is the discipline of *daily* exercise, even if you have to do a shortened or token version of your normal routine. This one improves suppleness and flexibility and is therefore usually painful – don't overdo it. It's best done in loose, little or no clothing.

Step 1 Stand, feet a foot or so apart, and attempt to touch your toes. Repeat three, five or ten times. It matters not a jot whether you can touch them or not – just push to feel that stretching of the lower back and the back of the knees. You can intersperse Step 1 with Step 2.

Step 2 Stand, reach for the sky, stretching upwards, hands above your head, rising on to tip-toe. Hold for five seconds. Repeat as Step 1.

Again, you should feel the stretching in arms, legs, neck and back. Try to deliberately stretch each bit of you from toes to legs to back to neck to arms to fingers.

Step 3 Stand, feet eighteen inches apart, hold both arms out straight in front, palms down. Now swing both arms round to the right as far as you can go, maintaining the position of arms (and legs). The right arm will reach much farther than the left pointing behind you. Now swing right round, still

153

holding the arms in position, to the left. Repeat five or ten times each side.

This is a twister.

Step 4 Kneel and sit on your heels, fold your arms *behind* your back and rotate your head clockwise, stretching your neck as much as possible. Then rotate anti-clockwise. Repeat three or five times.

Obviously one for the neck — a key tension point. Try to make sure you bend it down (so you can see your chest), up (so you can see the ceiling), and as far as possible to either side.

Step 5 Lie on your back on the floor. Use a book or towel to make your head comfortable. Raise your right leg, holding it straight, as far as you can. Lower it and repeat with the left leg. Repeat three, five or ten times.

One for the stomach. You can make this more strenuous if you like by turning it into trunk curls: you hook your feet under the bed or other low bar, put your hands behind your head and curl up as far as you can, keeping your legs straight.

These exercises are not meant to be strenuous, but form a convivial or meditative routine that you can get into the habit of doing. Unfortunately much of the competitiveness that abounds in management spills over into physical exercise and turns everything into Olympic-type efforts if we're not careful. THIS IS NOT A COMPETITION. However, in case you want something more demanding in the way of physical exercise, there are plenty of books available. This remains unashamedly a friendly book. We don't want to add to the distaste which many people still have for physical exercise due to being forced to do it at school. This led Winston Churchill to say, 'When I feel the urge to exercise, I lie down until it passes on.' Come to think of it, it didn't seem to do him much harm! Nonetheless we can say that physical exercise does most of us a lot of good as long as we don't compete or overdo it.

The next exercise is a physical one too, but this time it is about relaxing, which has quite a different feel from the first two.

RELAXATION

Step 1 Find a quiet place where you can sit comfortably but upright, both feet on the ground, head up, back straight.

Some people may like to do this cross-legged, or even lying down as in Step 5 of the previous routine, but you may be more comfortable in a chair.

Step 2 When you are comfortable, close your eyes and consciously relax all your muscles, starting at the top of your head, down through your forehead, ears, mouth, jaw, neck, shoulders and so on, going very slowly and becoming conscious of each muscle group as you go. Go right down to your toes.

Try to get into each group of muscles – be your neck, totally absorbed there before moving on. You can imagine that you're going deeper ... and deeper ... sinking down in warm water, or in a lift, or to the bottom of the sea. Take your time.

Step 3 Now begin to breathe in deeply through your nose and then out through your mouth. Listen to your breath come in ... and go out. ... Notice that there is a pause as you finish breathing out ... and before you begin to breathe in.

As you relax, you will find your breathing becoming shallower. Become very aware of your breathing and nothing else ... notice as it becomes slower, more restful.

Step 4 Continue breathing but begin to count backwards from ten to one in the pauses. So, breathe out – ten; breathe in – nine; breathe out – eight; breathe in – seven ... and so

155

on down to one, then back up to ten, down to one again and so on.

You can carry on like this for five, ten or even twenty minutes, concentrating wholly on your breathing. You may have stray thoughts but don't worry about them, just let them come and go.

With this exercise, like most of the others, you'll find you get better with practice. You can develop, with practice, what has been called the 'relaxation response' and be able to call upon this response even in stressful situations. This is an excellent survival tool which should be in every manager's briefcase.

MEDITATION

Meditation is similar to the 'relaxation response' in some ways – you need a daily discipline to get the most out of it, and you improve with practice. Meditation is the traditional Eastern route to self-knowledge and self-development and is a good way to reduce anxiety and tension, to improve clear thinking and to relax you. Many meditations involve the contemplation of objects, which is easier than contemplating words or ideas. Here is one meditation out of the many. Again, you need a quiet place in which to sit or lie down comfortably. . . .

Step 1 Choose a flower and place it in front of you.

Or pick any other object if you wish – a piece of jewellery, pottery or wood. The flower has the advantage of being alive and the rest of this exercise is based upon the flower – if you choose one of the other objects you'll have to improvise from now on!

Step 2 Note carefully all the characteristics of the flower – its colour, the shape of its petals, the markings, the texture. . . . Take your time. Study each aspect in turn, dwell upon it.

Step 3 Now think back from the flower to its beginnings as a seed. Think about the seed in the soil beginning to grow. Imagine the life forces in the seed, now asleep, now beginning to stir and awake. Imagine the seed shooting, pushing up from the earth, reaching for the light. Imagine the roots growing downwards into the earth seeking water and nutriments from the soil.

Step 4 Now see the shoot breaking into the air, opening out, receiving warmth and light from the sun, water from the dew and rain. See the buds developing and beginning to open out. Soon you have the flower you see before you.

Step 5 Now think on from the flower as it is. Imagine it reaching its peak of maturity and beginning to die down. Imagine the seeds being produced. See them fall to earth with the petals.

Now you are at the end and the beginning of the flower. As you go through the stages, see if you can imagine what it *feels* like to be that seed, that shoot, those roots, that flower. Feel, in Dylan Thomas's words, 'the force that through the green fuse drives the flower' as this life force is born, grows to maturity and dies away again.

There are many such meditations, as we have said, and this is just one example. As we have moved on from physical exercises to relaxation and meditation, however, it has become clearer how body and mind, physical and mental/emotional are not really separate at all but closely interlinked. These exercises start with maintaining and developing a healthy body but they also contribute to creating a healthy mind.

157

DEVELOPING A HEALTHY MIND

Balance is the key word here. A healthy mind is above all a balanced one. When we describe people as 'having their feet on the ground' or 'being together', we are noticing this quality in them.

A healthy mind is free from chronic fears and phobias *and* constant euphoria. The switchback of mania and depression is available to all of us under emotional or mental pressures – or we may tend to one pole or the other. While it is healthy to feel joy on a sunny day, fear and anxiety when you're in a difficult spot, or grief when someone you love leaves you, these feelings are normally transient, giving way to memory and equanimity as the events become part of us, part of our biographies.

You possess a sound or balanced mind when you are neither dogmatic and full of your own ideas *nor* over-reliant upon the ideas of other people. If you can listen to others and respect their views and yet disagree with them when you wish on the basis of your own clear and consistent views, then you have a 'balanced view' or an 'open mind'.

As often in this book, the key to the healthy mind lies not in this *or* that, but in *both* this *and* that. A balance must be kept between two equally desirable and complementary qualities which, if either were to exist alone, would become exaggerated and unhealthy. Take, for example, the balance needed between attention to detail and the ability to see the big picture. A healthy mind can deal with both – grasp the detail of the situation *and* get and retain an overview, a feel for the general principles involved. Getting 'bogged down in trivia' and always generalizing 'with your head in the clouds' are both consequences of doing *either or*; neither attitude is healthy.

To have a healthy mind you need a balance of feelings and emotions. We need to be aware of our feelings while not being overwhelmed by them. (We do not admire the professional exercising skill without compassion, any more than we admire the person disabled from acting by strong and uncontrolled emotions.)

158

Fear of being overwhelmed with feelings and being unable to cope with them often causes us to deny or repress those feelings – which, as we've said, is very unhealthy. A suppressed feeling often either comes out in an unhealthy way, possibly in losing one's temper, or builds up stress internally to the point where we succumb to one of the illnesses mentioned earlier.

For managers and professionals in particular there are various imbalances likely to happen in their lives which cause problems. Typical of these are imbalances between work and play; home and work; thinking and doing; material rewards and artistic or spiritual expression. These imbalances lead to excess on the one hand, impoverishment on the other. They may contribute to the break-up of families and relationships and cause considerable stress and, eventually, the lopsided development of the person. Managing yourself for a healthy mind and a balanced life is the first requirement for managing others in a healthy way.

The relaxation and meditation exercises described above will help you maintain and develop a balanced and healthy mind, and here are some others for practising mental and emotional health.

LOOKING AFTER YOURSELF

How do you deal with stressful situations? Your survival and development depend upon how well you cope – and this depends upon building up your repertoire of 'coping mechanisms'. Which of the following do you do?

1 Build up resistance through regular sleep, exercise ☐ and a healthy diet?

2 Talk through with your partner? ☐

3 Talk through with your boss or colleagues? ☐

4 Withdraw physically from the stressful situation? ☐

5 Practise relaxing or meditating? ☐

6 Give yourself breaks and treats when you need them? ☐

7 Strictly compartmentalize work and home life? ☐

8 Change to a different work activity? ☐

9 Change to a different non-work activity which engrosses you? ☐

10 Analyse the situation and plan a new strategy? ☐

11 Work harder and take work home? ☐

Score 2 points for each of the first 7 you ticked, and 1 point for any of the last 4 ticked.

The differential scoring system is based on the fact that the top seven coping mechanisms are generally reckoned to be better for you, although this varies from person to person. The fact that there are eleven items rather than the neat and tidy ten illustrates that this is not a complete list – can you think of any more you do? (*Award yourself 1 to 3 points depending upon how good this method is for you.*)

12 ☐

13 ☐

14 ☐

If you scored 12 or more points, then you've got a good repertoire of coping skills – you may still end up feeling stressed but you do know how to get help and to look after yourself.

If you scored between 6 and 12 points, you can cope to some extent, but you'd better start practising a few of these if you want to survive and develop more as a manager.

If you scored less than 6 points, you've got problems! Get help from a good 'coper' or a counsellor.

TREATS

We describe some people as being 'hard on themselves' or finding it difficult to forgive themselves for failures and disappointments. Many managers set themselves high standards which they inevitably fail to reach from time to time. Being able to treat yourself is the necessary balance to setting yourself high standards. High standards are a good thing but only in balance with the ability to pamper or reward yourself with little treats at appropriate times. 'Treats' are rewards or gifts you give yourself for hard work or hard times. They are often little things which give us great pleasure – a walk in the park at lunchtime, an hour with a favourite book, a drink at the end of a hard day.

Step 1 Write down all the ways in which you treat yourself.

1 _____
2 _____
3 _____
4 _____
5 _____
6 _____
etc.

Step 2 Look at your week (or day, month) and plan in some treats to reward yourself after tough meetings, hard days, unpleasant tasks, prodigious efforts etc.

Step 3 Make this a habit.

Stuck for ideas about treats? You can get lots of ideas by just asking your friends or work mates what they do. Once you get over the shyness you may feel in asking others about this, you'll find that everyone treats themselves from time to time – although some of us are much better at it than others! Never mind, you'll get better with practice.

(Here's a list of *some* of ours – we don't wish to seem too self-indulgent! – having a hot bath; washing my hair; taking the afternoon off to write letters or take a walk; going away for the weekend; doing the *Guardian* crossword with a special friend; *really* spending time with the kids; buying myself some flowers; having the occasional chocolate bar; finding a kitten to stroke; finding a person to hug; locking myself in the bathroom to get away from them all for ten minutes.)

It is often particularly important for *men* to learn how to treat and nurture themselves. We still live in a society that is split with regard to home and work. There is still 'women's work' and 'men's work', where men and women have been brought up to believe that women are the 'emotional specialists' and do the 'caring work' – bringing up children, looking after sick relatives and aged parents, nurturing husbands after hard days at the office. Women are often better at giving themselves treats, while many men are hampered by outdated attitudes and they may drive themselves and risk themselves without the relief and recreation of treats. This is just plain stupid; bad self-management and bad for managing in general. When you're good at giving yourself treats, you are more likely to give others treats too – again, something women may be better at than men.

Here's another everyday activity.

TALKING TO YOURSELF

Though held to be a sign of madness, this can be a good way of staying sane. If you do it out loud, however, it might be best to avoid busy offices! Talking to yourself or, perhaps, with yourself can get you in touch with your feelings and what might be called your 'inner voice' – your inner friend from Chapter 3. Again, this might be most useful when you are faced with a difficult problem or a frustrating or hurtful situation. In the absence of a supportive friend, you can counsel yourself.

Step 1 Find a quiet place to be with yourself.

This is most important even if you are going to talk to yourself silently. It is much better to speak to yourself out loud, although another way of doing it is to use a tape recorder. This has the advantage of preserving what you say, but it might make you too self-conscious. I like to do it while I'm out walking – talking out loud to myself, that is – although I get so absorbed in the conversation sometimes that I find I've walked right up to some startled fellow walkers, who edge past warily despite my cheery greeting!

Step 2 Tell yourself the story, explain the problem or describe the event.

Step 3 Now talk about the feelings you have about this problem or event.

Step 4 What possible courses of action are there? What are the options and their consequences?

Talking to yourself is a very healthy thing to do, although you have to have regard for other people's inhibitions! Older people often do this, and it is a sign of wisdom as well as lessened inhibition. The point is not to bottle things up or to rehearse things before they happen. If there's no one else to help, you can help yourself. You can try out new approaches to problems or deal with the bad feelings that might arise from unpleasant events – feelings that might fester inside you if you don't get them out.

The exercises in this chapter will help you to manage your health better. The key word is 'balance' – balance in diet, lifestyle, work and home, thought and action and so on. Some of the exercises also help with other aspects of managing yourself, for there is considerable overlap between managing your health and the three areas covered in other chapters on skills, action and identity. Equally, you will find further exercises in those chapters which will have a bearing upon healthy living, working and managing.

7 Working with other people

Managing yourself confronts you with a paradox: as soon as you take this personal responsibility, you need the help of other people more than ever. At first sight self-managing looks like DIY – doing it yourself. But when you get down to managing *you* – your survival, maintenance and development – it becomes clear how slim your resources are when standing alone. Relationships are the great arenas of development in human beings; we grow in the reciprocal giving and taking to and from each other. And, incidentally, the judiciary has long been aware of this – hence the punishment for people who con-spire ('breathe together') to commit a crime is often far greater than that for simply doing it on your own.

Managing yourself requires discipline. It requires both the support and the challenge to our own entrenched views which only other people can give us. Few of us can sustain the self-management effort on our own for very long. This is illustrated by experience from a large organization where we went a few years ago to help the managers develop themselves.

We carried out some informal research with a large company at which some fifty managers were given copies of a book of self-development activities[1] and invited to get on with some self-development on their own – to examine their practices, diagnose their strengths and weaknesses, and carry out some 'strengthening activities'. Two months later we went back to find out what had happened. We discovered some interesting facts

[1] M. J. Pedler, J. G. Burgoyne and T. H. Boydell, *A Manager's Guide to Self Development*, McGraw Hill, 1978, 1986. This is a workbook containing diagnostic frameworks and forty-two self-development activities.

which can be generalized far beyond this particular sample of managers. Four or five of these managers had made good progress, reporting significant steps forward in knowledge, skills or understanding – one engineer even kept the book by him, to work on in slack moments. On the other hand, at least as many could scarcely remember the book, and the great majority of the managers had read bits or all of it, but had not done anything with it – had not changed the way they managed as a result of it. On this evidence, we can posit a sort of Parkinsonian law:

> . . . that any attempt to make available unsupported self-development opportunities will result in 10 per cent of the people seizing the chance and making good use of it. On the other hand 90 per cent won't. Furthermore the 10 per cent we do reach happen to be the ones who are learning and self-developing anyway; they'll welcome the new opportunity but tend to be those in least need of it. . . .

So, an important part of managing yourself involves establishing sources of support, people and places, oases perhaps where you can go for rest and recuperation on the sometimes dispiriting journey. As well as support, you need help and comradeship from other resourceful human beings. This chapter is about harnessing and setting up these sources of support and help. We are suggesting methods or means, together with ideas for making a start on them:

- Finding a friend: working with a 'speaking partner'
- Finding allies: using your role set
- Making contacts: networking
- Getting comrades: setting up or joining a self-development group

All of these can be done within most organizations, although some are easier to do than others. You only need the cooperation of one other person to have a speaking partner, whereas setting up a self-development group is a more demanding venture. You can

165

also do these things outside the organization (except, perhaps, for using your role set). The important point is to ensure some method of support and help.

FINDING A FRIEND: WORKING WITH A 'SPEAKING PARTNER'

First and foremost, we need a good friend to help us manage ourselves. We need someone special to tell our good news to and to share bad experiences with. A 'speaking partner' is someone you meet from time to time to discuss how you are managing yourself. This may be someone at a similar point to you in their own development, but this is not always essential. For example, a younger manager may be fortunate enough to find an older person in the organization who is prepared to listen, question and offer the fruits of a longer experience.

In this case the older person would be acting as a mentor to the younger. This is a special and valuable example of a speaking partner. Another example could be two people who co-counsel each other, meeting at regular agreed intervals and splitting the time equally so that each acts as talker and listener in turns.

How do you choose a speaking partner? Probably your 'best mate' is not a good choice. You are too close and perhaps lack detachment. A good choice would be someone from another section or department whom you like or have met on a course or in the process of a project. If you recognize in that person someone who is also tackling the knotty problem of self-management or perhaps someone going through a crisis in their biography then they might be most appropriate. If you are youngish then an older person whose style you admire might be prepared to give you an hour or two every month. If you're still stuck, try the networking activity later in this chapter and see whether that suggests anyone. The main criterion is that the person should be interested and prepared to work with you over quite a period of time.

Once you have a partner, what do you talk about? Whatever

you wish; whatever problem, difficulty, interest or topic is relevant at this point to managing yourself. If you are following the ideas in this book then you will have no shortage of starting points. For example:

- entries in your personal journal or diary
- some action or changed way of doing things which you've been experimenting with
- a critical incident which has just happened – 'the most difficult (managerial) situation I've had to face in the last week, fortnight, month'
- something you've read
- something that's been on your mind – a worry, a nagging doubt

If you want to work well with a speaking partner it's a good idea to make sure you arrange the time and place properly. Meeting in the pub or for lunch might be a splendid way of warming up, but it may not be the best setting for good talking and listening. You need to find a suitable place and to book it for a suitable time, just like any other appointment or business meeting. Such a place might be a quiet corner with two comfortable chairs, or even a walk round the park where you can achieve the three objectives of *free talk*, *supportive listening* and *constructive responding*.

Free talking is simply feeling free and ready to talk about the issue or topic: free from distractions in the environment – telephones, interruptions, general noise – and ready in the sense of feeling this is the right time to talk about this, with this person. Readiness is a key principle in managing yourself – we can't do things unless we're ready to do them, and it is not a good idea to push ahead if you're not.

Supportive listening lies at the heart of a good relationship with a speaking partner.

Stop reading for a minute and just reflect on your own experience. Jot down on a piece of paper the names of three or

four people who have been helpful to you in the past. . . .
Now jot down what it was about each of those people that
made them helpful. . . .

The chances are that your list reads something like this:

- they were sympathetic and understanding
- they showed interest in what I was saying
- they respected me and my feelings
- they still liked me even when I made mistakes or did stupid things
- they sometimes challenged me and made me think
- they told me how they saw me, but in a way that helped me to listen to them

---

You may also have on your list that someone gave you helpful advice in the past; but you should be wary of the 'If I were you . . .' type of advice. It is nearly always most unhelpful for its purpose is to satisfy the speaker's needs to be of use, or to avoid getting into a difficult area, and not yours. It's little wonder that we very often ignore the advice given to us. In some ways this is a pity – everyone can look back on moments in their lives and say, 'I wish I'd listened to what old so and so said to me' – but often it is healthy because the aim of the speaking partnership is to help us generate our own solutions. In choosing our own path, judicious advice is often what we seek, but wise people give it very sparingly and accept it very cautiously. As Lao Tse said, it tends to be the case that 'the one who speaks does not know and the one who knows does not speak'.

As a supportive listener, the main aim is to try and manifest the qualities contained in the list above – to achieve those attitudes and actions which we have recognized as helpful to us.

Constructive responding is the twin to supportive listening and itself has two faces. The first of these is listening in silence and responding through silently paying attention to the speaker. Never

168

underestimate the value of silence in our rushed and overactive times. What many of us need most is the open space, the pool of silence in which we can reflect and be reflected. It's often during such silences that we hear our *inner* helper, our own *inner* voice, as discussed in Chapter 3.

Here's how to listen silently and with attention – a surprisingly rare occurrence between people but an easy skill to learn:

Agree a time limit with whoever is going to speak first – say ten minutes. Then show your interest and attention by looking your partner in the face. Keep a steady gaze of attention. Your partner will find it unnecessary to look at you all the time, they may look down, up, out of the window; but you will notice they glance back at you from time to time to check the attention. When you pay attention, do not speak. You are there to listen. Sit out the pauses, don't fill them. Nod if you absolutely must, and grunt if you feel you'll burst; but the main object is listening in silence and paying attention.

This gives the speaker an unusual opportunity for uninterrupted pursuit of a topic, a chance to explore a problem. In a surprisingly short piece of uninterrupted time a person can explore their thoughts and feelings and desire for action. Through the agency of a silent listener, who by being there and restraining her or his own desire to talk, a vessel is created in which the speaker can sort out ideas, clarify feelings and recognize wishes.

It may seem a bit unusual at first – because it is unusual. If you persevere and overcome the awkwardness of silences, you will find this an attainable skill, and a very valuable one to have acquired.

The other face of constructive responding is to act and intervene in various ways. Given the importance of silence and the danger of advice, you may by now feel you are between some Scylla and Charybdis, unable to say anything for fear of interfering rather than helping. Of course there are some important and helpful responses to make, as we all know. We must be emboldened to act, but skilfully – and skilful action is done in awareness of dangers, and with a sense of timing and readiness (see Chapter 5).

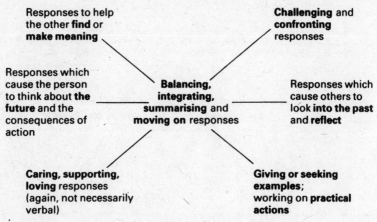

Figure 7.1

So, what sorts of responses are helpful? A simple sevenfold classification of these is shown in Figure 7.1. Very often these helpful responses involve questions to the speaker – usually prompting or 'open-ended', encouraging the other to talk or to take up a point as yet unexplored. Here are some examples of the sort of questions you might ask and responses you can try under these seven headings, all the time trying to be aware of what your partner is:

Thinking What is being said, the pattern of thoughts; is it logical? Detailed or general? In the past, present or future? Who is being talked about and who is not? What images and metaphors are being used? What assumptions does the speaker seem to be making?

Feeling What is the speaker feeling? Notice the gestures, posture, tone of voice, way of breathing and the expression of the face, eye movement.
Willing What does the person want to do? What is just a wish and what is a definite intention to act?

Remember the 'super senses' in Chapter 5? Applying these here leads to what we might call 'superlistening' to the way your partner responds to questions such as the following.

Category	Examples of questions or responses which may help your partner
1 Caring, supporting, loving responses	Pay close attention but don't stare. Show that you are listening and hearing with nods and smiles, but don't overdo it.
	Empathize. Say, 'If I were in your place I think I would feel ——' But don't *tell* the other person what they are feeling (although occasionally it can be preferable to say, 'Does that make you feel frightened/happy/jealous etc.?').
	Be warm and encouraging; give the other person positive feedback, e.g., 'I know you are good at ——, I saw you the other day', but don't get 'yucky' and overcomfortable.
	If you can do it naturally and your partner can receive it well, don't be afraid to touch, to take the other's hand or give them a hug. Nothing heals like hugging!
2 Challenging and confronting responses	Point out inconsistencies and contradictions in what your partner is saying, e.g., 'How consistent is what you've just said with the point you made five minutes ago?'

Look for inconsistencies between *words* and *feelings* and *actions*, e.g., 'You say you're not angry but you certainly look mad!'

Say what you really think is not right in what your partner is saying if you can do so straight and in terms of how *you* feel about it, e.g., 'I don't agree with your view of ——, it makes me feel angry.'

Give negative feedback in as supportive a way as possible, using 'I' statements, e.g., 'I feel attacked by you' rather than 'You are attacking me'. Remember that most of us can only handle one bit of negative feedback at a time.

3 Responses which help the other find meaning

Ask questions like:

'Can you see a pattern in all this, or a theme?'

'What is this saying to you?'

'Why is this happening to you?'

'What does this mean to you?' (But don't put your own meaning on events, and watch out for rationalizations.)

4 Giving examples, practical actions

Ask questions like:

'What sort of things are you talking about?'

'What type of person do you have difficulty with?'

'Can you give examples of other situations in which you feel helpless, angry, upset, etc?'

'What is your first step?'

'What resources will this require?'

5 *Responses which help the other reflect or look into the past*	*Ask questions like*:
	'Has this happened before?'
	'What did you do last time?'
	'Have you felt like this before?'
	'Give me some examples of incidents like this in the past.' (But don't get trapped in the past or in old guilt and 'If only . . .' sentiments.)
6 *Responses which cause the other person to think about the future and the consequences of action*	*Ask questions like*:
	'What do you want to do about this?'
	'What will be the consequences for yourself and all the others involved?'
	'What alternatives and options do you have?'
	'What blocks and obstacles are there?'
	'Where do you want to be with regard to this in two weeks/six months/a year's time?' (But watch for escapism into the future to avoid the present. Emphasize what can be done now, and move into the *practical action* area – 4 above.)
7 *Balancing, integrating, summarizing and moving on responses*	Watching the balance of the whole conversation with regard to analysis and action, past and present, thoughts and feelings, and trying to integrate them all.
	Being aware of your own thoughts, feelings and wishes – listening to yourself as the listener – and trying to remain detached and not allow these to influence what you are hearing from your partner. In particular,

173

is what you are doing/saying in any way being influenced by things *you* want from the other person?

Summarizing what your partner has said in order to get confirmation of points or to move things on.

Asking questions like, 'What shall we do now?' 'What is the next step [of the conversation]?'

Checking actions your partner has decided to do.

Introducing humour if things get too 'heavy'; lightness when things get too dark; warmth when it is needed.

This might look daunting, but don't be put off by the amount involved in listening. You can use this list to give you ideas to start with, or to review your efforts afterwards. Our aim is to help you improve your skills, but much more important than this is the simple human desire to help another person. You must have this before you can be a speaking partner because it gives you commitment to your partner, which is the first essential of the relationship. Once you've got this sorted out then just get going and have a bash, trying to improve as you go.

FINDING ALLIES: WORKING WITH YOUR ROLE SET

To survive in organizations we all need allies as well as friends. You may well be able to find such allies among your close colleagues at work – the members of your role set. This is the term applied to those people who occupy the roles or positions which relate directly to your role as manager, partner, friend or whatever. They include your boss, any colleagues with whom you have 'sideways' relationships and the people who report to you and for whom you are responsible, as well as your spouse, partner, children, family friends.

In a role set each role holder has obligations to and expectations of the person at the centre. You expect your boss to provide you with access to resources, a higher level of decision, to represent you elsewhere and so on. In return you have obligations to your boss – to manage a particular section, to report regularly and keep information flowing upwards and so on. Similarly with relationships outside of work.

A reciprocal exchange of obligations and expectations characterizes every role set. This web of relationships therefore puts all its members in a good position to judge the performance, skills, abilities and effectiveness of the person in the middle.

Of course, you may decide that because these are the people with whom you interact in your working life each day you don't want to risk disturbing the patterns by trying to enlist them in your self-managing efforts. On the other hand, if you take the initiative, it's highly likely that some of your role set will become interested too. If you establish a helping, developing relationship between you and some members of your role set, it is unlikely to stay as a one-way exercise. Others will become curious and want to know what you think of them and their performance on particular tasks, or in certain meetings, or in various aspects of your life together. If you decide that your role set members could help you with managing yourself, you are likely to create a little 'warm' spot where mutual self-help towards self-management is taking place.

ROLE SET ANALYSIS

First, we need to identify the people who hold the positions that make up your role set. For this exercise we will concentrate on a work-based set although, as we've made clear, you could focus on your set(s) outside work or, perhaps best, a combination.

Take a piece of paper and draw a circle in the middle to represent the role you occupy at work. Write your name under the title of your job. Then draw, around this centre circle, some other circles to represent all the 'significant others' in the role set of your job – those people with whom you probably have daily contact and who make demands on you and have expectations of you. For example, the role set of an office manager might look like Figure 7.2.

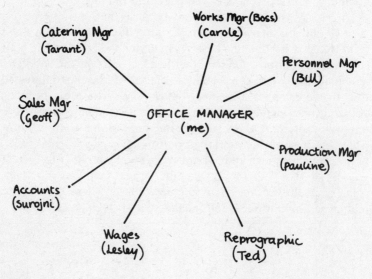

Figure 7.2

176

There can be as many people as you like. You can indicate closeness or regularity of contact by putting the circles near to yours or further away. You can indicate authority relationships by putting bosses above, colleagues to the side and those accountable to you, below.

The next thing to decide is how to enlist members of your role set to help you in your task of managing yourself. Whatever step you decide to take you will be introducing change into established relationships. You need to give some thought to the best way of doing this. To do it properly you have to overcome the barriers to open discussion and plain speaking which are caused by differences in authority levels. You have to manage this upwards, sideways and downwards.

Here are three ideas for starting this process of trying to tap the resources and knowledge of those people who see you at work every day.

'My expectations/your expectations'

Arrange an appointment with the people from your role set membership who you think might be able to help you or give you useful information. Then do a bit of preparation. For each person you want to meet, jot down the expectations that person has of you in your job and, in another column, the expectations you have of that person in their job. For example, taking the office manager again:

	Expectations of me	My expectations of her
Accounts supervisor (Surojni)	1 Fair loading of work. 2 Support for her actions with her people. 3 Personal support – to be available to listen.	1 Achieve work targets. 2 Deal with her own people problems. 3 Keep me informed about likely delays, trouble spots etc.

	Expectations of me	My expectations of her
4	To get resources for our departments.	4 Take initiatives – but let me know!
5	To represent her views to Carole, works manager.	... and so on ...
	... and so on ...	

When you meet the person concerned, you can either show them your 'homework' or say, 'I'd like to talk about how well I do my job in relation to yours' and just use this preparation as a shopping list. It depends on your relationship with that person and what it takes to get a *developmental* discussion going, i.e. one in which trust is established, new information is exchanged and personal change is made possible. In other cases presenting people with a piece of paper like this, especially if they are less senior, may alarm them into a superior–subordinate response – which will not give you what you need. Using your role set members to help you develop will only work if you can establish a developmental relationship, one where learning is the object, preferably for both parties.

If you can achieve this then you will have created a new speaking partner relationship for this exchange, and the earlier points about talking, listening and responding all apply.

'Kerbside conferences'

A more specific form of contract is that which you set up with one or more other people on a particular issue or occasion. Supposing you were worried about your performance in large meetings or unsure about negotiating contracts with other organizations and yet this was an important part of your job. If any of your role set members are in the same meeting or in a position to observe you in action, then there is an ideal opportunity for obtaining information from an outside observer to add to your own perceptions of how you did.

You can ask this member or members of your role set to look for particular things, to check any doubts you might have about your own performance. For example, you could say, 'I'd like you to look out for when I look lost or confused; what happens when the other person becomes aggressive; and how well I summarize what's going on.'

The next bit of the contract is to arrange a quick session afterwards to get that person's feedback on those three points. In selling, this is the 'kerbside conference' after every call, and it is a device that incorporates the best rules of skills development – try something with an observer watching and get feedback immediately afterwards.

Role set survey

A third idea is to survey all the members of your role set on how they see you operating or how they view the services offered by your department. This simply involves sending out a letter with an attached questionnaire requesting feedback on various aspects of your performance. Because of the relatively formal nature of the letter and questionnaire, you'll probably get a better response if you ask about the performance of your section or department (they're talking about you anyway!) than if you make it personal.

A suitable format might be:

Dear ——,
As you know, I'm trying to develop the services which the office supplies to the organization as a whole, and I'd like your views on what we do at the moment and any thoughts you might have on what we could do to improve the level of service.

I enclose a brief questionnaire and I'd be very pleased if you could return it to me by the 31st of this month.

Yours etc.

Working with Other People

The questionnaire should include such questions as:

1 What services do you expect from the office?

2 For each of the services you have listed in (1) above, please comment on each in terms of quality, grading it 'excellent', 'good', 'fair' or 'poor'.

3 What services which we currently do not provide would you like to see us put on in future?

4 What words would you use to describe the office? E.g. busy, relaxed, friendly, helpful, unhelpful, slow, bureaucratic, flexible, customer-oriented, time-wasters, skilful, useless etc. Please pick from these and add your own to give as full a picture as possible.

5 What words would you use to describe the management style of the office? E.g. autocratic, democratic, consultative, 'mushroom management', relaxed, task-oriented, people-centred etc. Please add words of your own.

This survey might give you more impersonal details about the performance of your section than personal data about you. However it will create an important opening and opportunity to go and talk in more detail with each or any respondent. Even if you do not have high hopes about the value of such survey data, you might try the exercise in order to make these openings possible. After all, it's much easier to go in and say, 'I'd like to chat about your comments to my survey questions' than it is to go in cold and say, 'Well, what do you think of the way I manage'!

MAKING CONTACTS: NETWORKING

As well as friends and allies, it helps to have lots of contacts. An idea that extends outside work is your personal support network. Networks are the informal organizations that exist between people with similar interests or who like each other's company. Networks act as grapevines; they convey gossip and information often much more quickly than formal systems of communication. Knowing where to go to get information is one of the most important political skills; in work organization, for example, people such as receptionists and catering staff often have all sorts of information because they come into contact with so many people. As everyone knows, the 'old boy network' operates to help its, usually male, members get on and get things done. A support and development network can operate in a similar way except that the goals are different. The aims of such a network are not preferment and 'backdoor' manoeuvring but mutual help with self-management.

NETWORKING

Begin by identifying the extent and membership of your support network. In the table below we've listed some valuable dimensions of support. Write down against these the names of the people you can call on for help on this dimension. Who does these things for you? To remind you that networks for support, and development, and self-management extend way beyond the work organization, there are two columns for people's names — 'at work' and 'outside work':

Dimensions of support	Names of people you can go to for this kind of support and help	
	At work	Outside work
Who . . .		
. . . do I enjoy chatting with?		
. . . do I go to coffee and lunch with?		
. . . cheers me up?		
. . . makes me feel competent and valued?		
. . . can I discuss my self-management with?		
. . . Can I talk to about the exercises in this book?		
. . . can I share good news with?		
. . . can I share bad news with?		
. . . do I get useful information from?		
. . . 'gives it to me straight' i.e. gives me feedback?		
. . . challenges me to action?		
. . . can I depend on in a crisis?		

182

Look at your list of names. Do you have a lot of gaps? Do you get all your support at home and not at work or vice versa? Do you rely heavily on one or two people or have you got a wide spread of people in your network?

You will probably have some gaps in your list, which is normal; but having a wide range of people to call upon adds immeasurably to our resourcefulness. A network, remember, is composed of interconnected points. Imagine a string bag. Any one point is only connected to four other points, but *through* those four, each point can reach eight others, and through those twelve more, and so it goes on. When faced by a problem to which we don't have the answer, we ring up the person we know who is most likely to know. He or she may know or not, and if not, they probably know someone else (whom we don't know personally) who might know . . . and so it goes on.

Networking is an important activity for self-managers. You will need all sorts of help, and the bigger and more varied the network of people you have to call upon, the better supported you will be. Of course, you in turn will become a source of support, help and information for other people, because you know so many people. . . . To build up and enlarge your support network will take time and a commitment to other people's needs as well as your own. But helping other people to manage themselves is one of the best ways of developing yourself.

GETTING COMRADES: SELF-MANAGEMENT GROUPS

According to Bernard Lievegoed,[1] this is the age of the group; and Roger Harrison[2] tells us that one of the main characteristics of 'New Age' thinking is to join a group. Friends, allies and contacts might become comrades if they joined with you in a group to tackle together the quest for self-managing. The tailor-made form of working with others on your self-development and self-managing is to belong to a group dedicated to that purpose. There is no fixed pattern to such groups but our recent research showed them to consist typically of six to ten members, meeting regularly (at weekly, fortnightly, monthly intervals) for a half day or a day at a time over a relatively long period – from six months to two years or more.[3] Sometimes such groups 'grow' out of courses or project teams where people want to carry on working together.

Sometimes self-development groups are 'facilitated' by a trainer, and it helps if some members have access to training ideas and resources. However the main requirements are the commitment to your own self-management and an agreement to work together for mutual help and to learn with and from each other. All for one and one for all. The group might be an oasis to retreat to, or a pressure cooker for development; or it might be both at different times. (Remember the 'clover leaf' of surviving, developing, getting ready, shown in Figure 1.4?) At its best there is a strong sense of comradeship and a sense of purpose.

Here are some guidelines and exercises for setting up and managing a group. The main phases of a group's life are:

[1] *Towards the 21st Century*, Steiner Book Centre, Vancouver, Canada, 1979.

[2] 'Strategies for a New Age', *Human Resource Management* 22(3), Fall 1983.

[3] M. J. Pedler *et al.*, *Self Development Groups for Managers*, Manpower Services Commission, Sheffield, 1984.

1 Setting up and recruiting.
2 Getting started – the first meeting.
3 Choosing a focus.
4 Decision-making.
5 Maintaining energy and commitment.
6 Helpful actions.
7 Reviewing progress.
8 Closing down.

1 SETTING UP AND RECRUITING

Groups can be formed from members of the same organization, from professional networks or from any common interest group. Depending upon your choice, there are three ways of making contact with other, interested people:

Personal invitation by letter. For example:

Dear Alison,

As you know, I have been working on ways of improving my managing skills and I want to continue in the company of other interested people. I'd like to invite you to a discussion meeting in my office on 22nd January at 10 a.m. to consider setting up a 'self-development group'. This is a 'no obligation' meeting – each person will have a choice to make at the end – 'Yes, I'd like to join' or 'No, thanks, not for me at this time'! I think a small group of six or eight of us meeting perhaps every three weeks for a few hours to share ideas, learn new skills and generally tackle problems facing us, could be of benefit to us all.

Please let me know if you can come.

Announcement. You can put up a notice on a notice board or in a newsletter inviting others to contact you or join you for a

185

discussion meeting. It is a good idea to have an open meeting with no obligation to join to begin with. This gives everyone a chance to ask questions and make up their own minds.

Invite another person. If you know three or four people who might like this sort of experience you can contact them personally and ask them to bring one other person along to the first meeting.

It's essential that people are free to choose to join the group or not. Voluntary commitment is very important if it is to work; after all, it is meant to be self-management! 'Invitations' can sometimes pressurize people, so be careful.

2 GETTING STARTED – THE FIRST MEETING

The first step after having held your open discussion and got six to ten members or so, is to break the ice at the first meeting proper and begin to establish the openness and trust among members that will help you get down to work.

The best way to start building trust is to get members to share things about themselves – their lives, their interests and their concerns or problems. Here are three ways to get started on sharing information:

Introduction pairs. Members of the group pair off and 'interview' each other, asking whatever questions they like about work, home, hobbies, beliefs, why they have come to the group and so on. Allow ten minutes each way. After twenty minutes the group re-convenes and each member introduces their partner (not themselves) to the group, saying, 'I've been talking to Jack who is . . .'

When each person has been introduced in this way, the whole group can discuss similarities and differences.

Glimpses

Step 1 Each person writes down on a piece of paper ten important things about themselves.

Step 2 In turns members come to the blackboard or flipchart and write up the items on their list. They can do this without comment or by explaining them and saying a bit more about them as they go down. Others can ask questions as long as this is okay by everyone.

You can then have a discussion on how different people present themselves – who is complimentary and who is self-denigratory and so on. What sort of people emerge from these glimpses?

A variation on this activity is to ask each person to write down two lists in step 1: 'ten important things about myself which I find easy to tell others' and 'ten important things about myself that I find difficult to tell others about'. People then think about their two lists for a few minutes, and at step 2 pick out of the twenty items, ten to write up. Obviously they can, if they wish, stick entirely to the first list. However most of us don't, so this variation can encourage a bit of risk-taking.

You can also take this a step further with 'some ways in which I think *other* people see me'.

A letter to the group

Step 1 All members write a letter introducing themselves and addressed to the rest of the group. The letter can take various forms. It can be in the first person, introducing oneself – 'My name is ——, I am ——' etc. Alternatively it can be in the third person as though the writer were describing somebody else – 'I am writing to introduce —— He/She is ——' etc. This is like giving a reference for someone, so you could look upon this alternative in that light.

Step 2 When the letters have been written, each person takes it in turn to read theirs out to the group. Alternatively, one

187

person can collect them and read them all out omitting the person's name. Members have to guess who wrote each letter. A third way of doing it is to fold the letters into a hat and for each person to read one out either including or omitting the name as they wish.

The exercise can be good fun, and once again can lead into a discussion about how we see ourselves and how we present ourselves to other people. It is also good practice at trying to stand aside and view oneself objectively, for being able to observe oneself in action as it were is an important aspect of self-management.

3 CHOOSING A FOCUS

Getting to know one another and learning something about all the members of the group is quite enough work for the first meeting. However, managers are notoriously keen on getting down to work, and it will soon become necessary to decide what to work on. There are various strategies you can follow, depending upon the needs of members. Self-management groups usually focus on one or more of the following:

Tackling members' work problems.

Looking at 'here and now' issues of what's going off in this group – communication, decision-making etc.

Structured exercises. Members work on activities brought along by other members, e.g. like the ones in this book.

Personal life concerns. Members look at issues in their lives as a whole.

'How I manage', where the group works with members talking about how they manage in particular situations.

Here are a couple of ways of arriving at the needs and interests of members in order to choose a focus.

Needs and offers

Step 1 All members have two postcards, one headed 'needs' and the other 'offers'. Each writes down *three* needs they have as a manager and/or as a person; and three offers of knowledge, skill, help they could make to other group members.

Step 2 Pin up the postcards on the wall under 'Help Wanted' and 'Help Offered' notices. When everyone has read them, see if there are:

● any matching needs and offers
● any common needs
● any patterns of needs and offers

From the needs displayed the group can pick a starting point and begin work, focusing on the person with the need.

Critical incidents

Step 1 Each member agrees to note down, each day between the first and the next meeting, 'the most difficult managerial task/problem I had to tackle today'.

Step 2 Members take it in turn to read out their 'difficult tasks/problems' and how they dealt with them. Other members say how they would have tackled similar issues.

Of course, you may not need these exercises to help you start. Members may be able to put their problems and difficulties straight on the table. Most of us need to warm up a little, however.

4 DECISION-MAKING

Deciding where to start and what to do next is always difficult. Arriving at a consensus is best, but often some people don't mind what happens next, while others may be pulling in different directions. Sorting this out takes time and some people get impatient and frustrated. Try to:

189

(a) make sure *everyone* says what they want
(b) write all possible options on a board or flipchart paper to help everyone make personal choices and take a collective decision
(c) *Don't* assume silence means consent. It usually doesn't.
(d) *Do* review decisions made at the end of the session – how do we feel about them?

In the end recognize that a good group meets the needs of *all* its members. If we do X now, we'll remember to do Y later.

5 MAINTAINING ENERGY AND COMMITMENT

Energy goes up and down in a group, just as in life. Don't expect to be boiling over all the time, being quiet and reflective is just as valuable and necessary at times.

If, however, you feel energy and commitment are flagging, don't let it drag on. Bring the question up. Say that you feel 'bored', 'low' etc. and ask how others feel. If others feel as you do, try a different activity, a change of pace or place. Go for coffee, jump up and down or something.

6 HELPFUL ACTIONS

Being helpful isn't always as easy as it sounds. A lot of 'help' isn't helpful, but makes the problem worse. Here are some things which are helpful in most groups.

(a) Respect other people's boundaries. Allow them their defences just as you want to keep yours. *But* at the same time don't be afraid to give someone a little push or pull if you think they want to go a bit further, say a bit more.
(b) Give each person as much time to speak as they want. Try to decide when to move on and when to keep the focus on that person. It's not enough to take what the person says at face value: 'I think it is someone else's turn now' may mean 'I'm finding this difficult, can someone help'.

Whereas in a normal discussion meeting we may follow a *topic*, with everybody chipping in as and when, in a group we follow the *person*. Have they finished speaking? Have they had enough time? Do they want to go further?

(c) People need a combination of *support* and *challenge* to develop. Warm baths of support are lovely, but we don't want to move out of them. Challenges to our ways of thinking and acting are stimulating but tiring too – we can only take so much of it. Is everyone getting supported *and* challenged?

(d) Silences. Learn to live with them and don't be rushed into filling them. A silence may allow someone to sort something out in a way which talking can't.

(e) Helping people decide what to do about a problem or situation is often difficult. Listening is perhaps the most useful thing we can do (see above) and after that getting people to commit themselves to an action before the next meeting (few things are more healing or encouraging than the first small step down a long, long road – see Chapter 2). Get the person with a problem to say what their next step will be before you go on to the next topic/person. At the next meeting check back and find out what happened.

There are three essential 'human rights' with regard to communication in a self-management group:

● the right to speak
● the right to be listened to
● the right to remain silent

At the very least, each person should feel able to speak freely and to take up 'air time' in the group. Secondly, each person should be right to expect sympathetic listening and questioning to enable them to express what he or she wants to say. This is important because we often do not have the

191

words to say what we want to say, and because it is sometimes hard for us to be open about certain things. Thirdly, everyone should have the right to remain silent. But do check out what their silence means; silence does *not* always mean consent or that the person is comfortable. Find out.

7 REVIEWING PROGRESS

If you have worries about energy, commitment or whether the group is meeting the needs of its members then this is a good time to review the progress of the group. In fact a regular review of progress is a good idea – perhaps every second or third meeting – to check direction and take corrective action if necessary.

There are several ways of reviewing progress. The simplest is to spend the last few minutes of the meeting with each member giving their evaluation and views of the proceedings. Another way is to 'brainstorm' a joint list of what is helping the group and what is hindering. Get someone to act as scribe and just shout out as many things as you can. Discuss them all individually and decide what actions to take, especially on the hindrances, but also to increase the 'helping' forces.

You can also do a simple questionnaire to test members' feelings. Here is an example:

1 What are you getting from these group sessions?
2 What are you giving to other members?
3 Is the level of trust in the group high or low?
4 Does everyone participate and get a fair share of 'air time'?
5 Does the group have a clear sense of purpose?
6 Taking each member of the group in turn, what would you like to see them continue to do, stop doing or start doing? E.g.:

Name	Continue to do	Stop doing	Start doing
Bill			
Joan			
Ellen			
Eversley			

7 What would you like to see changed or done differently?

When each person has filled this out, the answers can be read out or collated on a chart. Alternatively you can just discuss without revealing detailed answers, the value of the questionnaire being in focusing everyone's thoughts on the key issues and allowing for some thinking time.

8 CLOSING DOWN

Often a very difficult thing to do. Some members may want to continue while others don't. The worst thing to happen is the 'creeping death' of members dropping off gradually and individually. It is much better to decide to finish on a given date and have a little celebration – a meal or a party – to mark the occasion.

At the last meeting you can do a full review of what members have gained, and allow time for some last messages between people. Is there any unfinished business? Dealing with these matters and the whole question of closing may make some members feel awkward and want to avoid it, but it is important to close properly – to make a good end.

Self-development groups can be quite daunting in prospect because we tend to be used to 'teachers' or 'trainers' organizing our learning and development for us. Depending on how you feel, you may be able to enlist the help of your management development or training people, to help with setting up and running a self-development group.

CONCLUSION

Finding friends, allies, contacts and comrades has been the theme of this chapter. Working with people as speaking partners, in our role sets, networks or in groups is important in reducing the isolation we may feel if trying to go it alone. We need other people most when we take the responsibility for managing ourselves.

193

They can help us release our own energy and overcome our tendencies to get blocked and demoralized or stuck in the grooves and ruts of work organizations. The effects of people developing or taking initiatives to manage themselves can be very contagious. Where two or three or more band together for these purposes they create warm spots in the organization which begin to heat up the rest. The opposite is also true – that the influence of lots of stuck, isolated or non-developing people in the organization can deaden and stiffen everyone.

The development 'climate' of an organization forms the environment in which the manager manages and develops (or not). Creating a climate that supports self-management and development is a natural and desirable extension of the theme of this chapter – managing yourself with the help of other people. It is to the question of how to build the 'developing organization' that we turn our attention in the next chapter.

8 Managing yourself within the organization

Working with friends, allies, contacts and comrades is the obvious starting point for managing yourself within the organization. Beyond personal connections, however, there are some wider issues of great importance related to the organization as a whole. In this chapter we consider three main aspects of organizations and provide you with some frameworks for analysis and action.

The first aspect concerns the *stage of development* of the organization. We can talk of organizations developing through a series of stages or phases, each of which is characterized by particular needs or tasks to be accomplished – just as we can talk about these things in individual lives. Different demands are made upon people depending upon the current stage of development of the organization; different values are in force and particular qualities are called for to contribute to the particular tasks in hand.

Secondly, and following on, is the matter of the *organizational climate*. What are the characteristics and quality of this climate? How well does it support individuals in their self-management? Are people's efforts to make choices and take initiatives discouraged or rewarded? It is one thing to embark on managing yourself in a supportive climate and quite another matter where the climate is oppressive, unsupportive and generally unhelpful.

This brings us to our third theme in this chapter – *what can you do to manage yourself in a non-supportive organizational climate*? How can you find energy and resources in an arid and infertile organization? Managing yourself is clearly much more difficult under these circumstances. You have to take the initiative even

195

more strongly, become an 'entrepreneur'; yet there is no encouragement and the cold clasp of the organization's climate outside chills us inside and drains our courage and enthusiasm.

Before going into detail on these three issues, let's backtrack a little to clarify the perspective of this chapter, and indeed of the whole book. Managing yourself within the organization is another step along the road we began in Chapter 1 – managing ME first and working outwards to other people.

MANAGING FROM THE INSIDE OUT AND FROM THE BOTTOM UP

A few years ago we used to hear a great deal about 'organization development' as a body of methods for helping people in organizations to cope with change. 'OD', as it was known, operated 'top-down', the first requirement being to enlist the support and involvement of top management, who, through project steering groups, maintained an overview of all the change efforts which then 'trickled down' into the organization. Today, although organizations are no less beset by change and turbulent environments, we seem to hear less about 'OD'. One reason is that working through the existing authority structure does little to release the energy and initiative of people lower down. If energy is blocked up within the organization, it is because people in the middle and lower reaches feel oppressed by the weight of those above them. A 'top-down' change effort is experienced as just another example of being told what to do, and is usually viewed with suspicion or apathy. By its very nature, its inbuilt paradox – 'I order you to be democratic; be free or else' – contains the seeds of its own almost inevitable failure.

The perspective of this book is that taking initiatives and making changes has to start inside and work outwards. It is this inside-out, managing-me-first process which creates energy and warmth which radiates outwards and begins to rise up within the organization. This 'rising-up' development needs helpers and expertise on tap and not on top.

In Chapter 1 we spoke of the problem of 'stuckness' within the organization – of people stuck in limited jobs, with limited horizons, bored, working without enthusiasm and commitment or simply 'gone to ground'. Stuckness is the energy crisis of the 1980s. Less visible than the fuel crisis of the 1970s because it dwells inside each one of us, its effects are even more far-reaching. When we're stuck we feel powerless, unable to influence events. We tick over, at best on half power, not using a tenth of our energies and creativity. It doesn't feel good either, quite apart from the economic and organizational effects. While feeling this awful stuckness, each of us has at the same time an urge to use our abilities, to exert ourselves, to exercise our full powers of awareness and competence.

Of course blame for this state of affairs cannot be laid entirely at the door of the organization we happen to work for. The truly awful problems of the world outside press in upon us, are brought to us nightly on the TV screen. I should be doing something to help – but what can I do? Modern consciousness can be painful. We live very outer-directed lives while being aware that much of what we do is trivial. Our appetite for material things seems insatiable, yet they satisfy less and less. We are conscious of inner tensions between what we say and what we actually do; between what we believe in and how we live; between what we do and what we could do. These inner splits are mirrored in the outer absurdities of our time where Africans starve as Europeans destroy surplus food; where the rich countries sell arms to poor ones in order to make peace; where tobacco companies sell disease and death in order to maximize profits.

Managers, like other people, are prey to these feelings of inadequacy and helplessness. There are two choices. We can batten down the hatches and keep our heads low – trying to survive and maintain ourselves in hope of better times, relying on our gallant captain to see us through, kept going by promises of 'jam tomorrow' and blaming others when things go wrong – or *we* can try to develop out of the recession/depression. Merely to try and suppress the pain, trying not to see the problems, can only be a

197

short-term measure. There are striking parallels between some of the organizational problems – bigness, inflexibility, wastefulness, impersonality and even inhumanity – and those that we can see operating at the global level. This is another example of a principle we've noted earlier, that of the interconnectedness of inner and outer; in this case between what is happening in the organization and what is happening outside. Once we can see this then it offers a way forward, for if the inside and the outside are connected, then to work on one is to affect the other.

Feelings of helplessness in the face of the world's problems lessen if we can begin to work on a different form of relationship inside the organization; in a cold and hostile organization we must perhaps turn our attention outside, to make a contribution there. Wherever we make a start, it is down to each of us to take the initiative, for we seem to have reached a time when the efforts of large entities – corporations, governments – are all too often blocked or perverted. There are too many egotistical and incompetent captains about. We can no longer trust them to sort it out for us or to act responsibly on our behalf; it is we who have to start managing, ourselves first and then others, starting at the bottom, working upwards to the top.

WHAT IS YOUR ORGANIZATION'S STAGE OF DEVELOPMENT?

Organizations are dynamic. Things do not stay the same and in recent history there has never been a time when this was more obvious. As 'household name' companies are being merged, or simply dying, at the other end of the life cycle new small businesses and cooperatives are springing up. The interconnection of these two ends of the life cycle is obvious. Without the collapse of the large manufacturing organizations on which we have come to rely for jobs and wealth, there could be no new life in the forms we are now experiencing. Moving through these stages is a traumatic and painful process especially for those suddenly thrown out of

198

employment and with little support and encouragement for what comes next. Yet this is a process we should be able to understand because birth, death and the intervening stages are part of the organizational life cycle. Organizations, like human beings, are unique and face particular problems and circumstances. At the same time there are some typical problems and questions which most organizations seem to face at certain times. These issues relate to the stage of development of the organization. For example, a company which establishes standard rules and systems to create a consistency of quality and treatment subsequently begins to experience problems of rigidity, lack of motivation and complaints from unit managers about their lack of autonomy. When these problems reach a significant level they have to be dealt with, and these actions, while resolving the old problems, also create the conditions in which the new ones will arise. This is the cycle of development: taking the next step; dealing with the 'now' problems within the context of a life cycle.

In the table below, we have mapped out six typical stages in the life cycle of the organization, together with the problems and issues which tend to arise at each of these stages. Can you spot your organization and its current problems and tasks?

Table 8.1

Stage of development of the organization	Typical tasks and problems associated with this stage
1 The new business – starting a new organization, either as an independent entrepreneur, or as in a new department or section within an existing enterprise.	What is the vision of the new organization? What will it look like, what will it do, what will it feel like? How can this version be turned into action? What resources are needed? Where will the premises, equipment, money and people come from? How can we market ourselves and begin to trade with the wider world?

2 The pioneer organization – small with a dynamic, pioneering leader or initiating group.

Do we continue small or grow larger?

If we expand, what new systems are needed to cope with increased business?

How will new people be integrated? How will the initiators and the 'in-comers' work together?

Succession. Who can replace the leader or the initiators? Is a new style of leadership needed?

3 The expanding organization – the independent enterprise or section gets bigger and more complex.

Doubts arise about the pioneers. There are questions about competence and grumbled about authoritarianism. Times are changing and the way we used to do things is no longer appropriate.

What new systems are needed to bring order to the hitherto creative chaos?

How can 'scientific management' methods be implemented to ensure standardization, consistency and control?

What specialist functions need to be established, e.g. sales, administration, research, personnel?

4 The established organization – which has been formalized for some time, with written procedures and logical, scientific method applied to most aspects of its functioning.

How can we deal with the problems of rigidity and inflexibility, red tape and bureaucracy that have set in?

Why is there so much apathy and low motivation about?

What can be done about the rivalry and competition between departments and functions which should be expended on production, sales and competing in the market?

Can we decentralize and differentiate – to give more autonomy?

5 *The 'wilderness organization'* – one which has lost its way and got out of touch with the outside world. This is increasingly likely with advancing age and size, especially in the case of bureaucracies.

How can we change our relationship with our customers and clients? Should we have new clients?

Can we decentralize and differentiate to meet customer needs?

How can we change our unhealthy view of the outside world, including our customers, the community and the environment, from one which almost sees these as 'enemies' or obstructions to be bullied, cajoled and overcome, by trickery and sharp practice, if necessary?

What should be our new moral purpose? What would build a healthy relationship, i.e. one of mutually advantageous collaboration with other stakeholders including the government, customers, community?

6 *The dying organization* – one that has failed or gone bankrupt, or whose initial mission is finished and which can/should no longer continue.

Can anything be done to reverse the failure? Can the organization be rescued through merger, 'surgery', 'buyout' or other means, to create new life, a new mission and a fresh start?

Should anything be done to reverse the death process, or is this natural and indeed desirable?

What can be done to come to a good end? How can closing down be made as positive and as painfree as possible?

What are the moral obligations to the stakeholders – employees, customers, shareholders and community?

What new seeds can spring from the husk of the old organization?

What are the implications of your organization's current stage of development for you? How can you survive and protect yourself in this dynamic environment and prepare and develop in order to make a contribution to some of the critical tasks at this time?

Start by locating your organization in Table 8.1. In broad terms, which description of typical tasks and problems best fits your organization or department? Take some time to jot down the specific issues which you see your organization facing. You may see these as problems to overcome or as tasks to be accomplished. The general list in the right-hand column of Table 8.1 may help, but list your own specific items here:

QUESTIONS, PROBLEMS OR TASKS FACING MY ORGANIZATION NOW

1 _____

2 _____

3 _____

etc. _____

When you've made your list, put down, against each one, the qualities or skills of people, and perhaps the ways of working, which will help with these tasks:

QUALITIES, SKILLS AND WAYS OF WORKING WHICH WILL HELP WITH CURRENT CRITICAL TASKS

1 _____

2 _____

3 _____

etc. _____

You could show these lists to other people to get some idea of how they see the situation. Thinking about these should give you a better idea of where your organization is and where you fit in. It should also tell you whether your abilities and ways of working belong more to the past, present or future. A few examples will illustrate this.

In the early stages of starting up a new business, people are needed with imagination and commitment who don't mind 'roughing it', will work all hours and are prepared to see rewards in the future. Inventive people who can turn their hands to whatever comes up respond flexibly and quickly in these early stages.

After a time, though, some order is needed. This means that people with quite different qualities are required – specialists who can divide work up and establish tight controls and standards over work areas. Professional competence replaces the Jacks-of-all-trades. Again, though, after a time things start to go wrong. The established organization needs people who can shake up structures that have become rigid and arthritic due to demarcation, division of labour, specialization and bureaucracy. Now people are wanted who can work across boundaries, who have 'people skills' and are good trainers and negotiators.

In the 'wilderness organization', inward-lookingness has become the major problem and people are urgently needed who can look outside and work into the community to change the relationship between the organization and the wider world. And in the final stages, this need for people who can be the midwives of new initiatives becomes even more urgent. Counsellors and caretakers become key figures.

These few examples of the qualities and ways of working appropriate at given stages of organization development help to explain why so many people get beached or stuck even in quite senior positions. We wonder how on earth old so-and-so ever managed to get that job! The 'Peter Principle' holds that such people proved themselves competent at lower levels and were promoted until they eventually reached a level of incompetence where they then stuck. But many people got promoted because their skills and abilities were relevant to the problems of the organization at a given time, at a particular stage in its development, and now, because of the development cycle, have become less valued and useful. The trappings of their offices now look like rewards for old deeds. At any given time there will be people whose qualities match the needs of that time, and, indeed, those whose time has not yet come. For all of us, unless we can learn new skills and ways of working, the time will eventually pass.

Those whose time is past are part of the 'stuckness' problem, but those ahead of their time constitute a different problem. Such people are often either unrecognized – disguised as 'regular guys' – or are mavericks, cavorting on the fringes of the organization and its policies. They tend to do their own thing, not necessarily making much of a contribution to the development of the organization. Yet ironically the organization's future may depend upon harnessing the ideas and talents of these mavericks. Many organizations are currently in stages 4 and 5 of our model, desperately trying to move from centralization and standardization to local control and delegation of power. Ironically, their solution is often highly regressive – appoint a 'strong man' (sic) to put it all right – i.e., attempt a false or distorted return to the pioneer stage. In this situation, what they in fact urgently need is the energies and ideas of people who have learned to manage themselves, who take personal responsibility and initiatives, to help with the next step.

Whether the mavericks can be whipped in and rounded up is open to question. They have developed their idiosyncratic styles (for 'lifestyle' rather than 'professional competence', let alone 'organizational loyalty' tends to be what they value) while the organization has been trying to encourage one single managerial style. They have often defined their style to counter what they see as the shortcomings of being a 'good company X man' which is what all the training courses and recent managerial exhortations have been aimed at. Such people are individualistic, pursuing their own goals irrespective of those of the organization. Sometimes they become celebrated characters or 'mascots' and in doing so display the potential energy not being tapped by the organization with its central controls and standards which do not support the self-managing impulse. Often they are much more highly valued outside their organizations than within them – 'prophets in their own country'.

The problem here is one of trying to balance appropriate organization while empowering people to develop themselves and take initiatives. As always in the development process, it is not just *this* or *that*, but *both* this *and* that. It is not a question of bureaucracy or self-management, but coherent organization and having people who take responsibility for themselves.

SO WHAT'S THE CLIMATE LIKE IN YOUR ORGANIZATION?

Whether the mavericks can be rounded up and whether other people are encouraged to manage themselves depends upon the climate prevailing in your organization. If you can spot some mavericks around, then this at least indicates a degree of clemency without which these half-hardy varieties could not survive!

We use the word climate in its original sense of 'weather conditions' – which support or inhibit the growth of particular forms of life – and as in the 'climate of opinion' – the sum of people's attitudes, prejudices and views on what is okay and not okay in the organization. The climate arises out of the history, traditions, locations, structures and technologies of the organization and yet is less concrete than these largely visible features. Partly stemming from the physical environment and affecting and being affected by the social life and procedural norms, it comes through as a pervasive tone or 'feel'.

In terms of warming people up and encouraging them to take the initiative in managing themselves, the prevailing climate is the critical factor. It is closely related to and partly determined by the current stage of development of the organization. In managing yourself within the organization, assessing the climate is the next step after considering this current developmental stage. It is the next level of microscopic analysis, if you like.

SELF-MANAGING CLIMATE QUESTIONNAIRE

Here is a questionnaire which helps you to identify what the conditions are like in your organization in terms of various aspects or dimensions of the climate. Go through the following ten dimensions and locate your organization or department on each of them, ringing the number, from 1 to 7, to represent where you see the climate in this respect.

1 Physical aspects. The amount and quality of space and privacy afforded to people; the temperature, ventilation, noise and comfort levels.

People are cramped for space, with little privacy and poor surroundings.	1 2 3 4 5 6 7	People have plenty of space, privacy and good physical conditions for managing themselves.

2 Learning resources. The numbers, quality and availability of books, films, training packages, equipment, training staff and other resources for learning.

Very few or no resources; out-of-date and neglected equipment; only technical trainers.	1 2 3 4 5 6 7	Many resources — packages, films, books etc; up-to-date and well-maintained equipment; many training staff.

206

3 Encouragement to learn. The extent to which the members of the organization feel encouraged to try new things, take risks, experiment and learn new ways to do old tasks.

No encourage-ment to learn; no expectations placed upon people to learn new skills and knowledge.	1 2 3 4 5 6 7	Members are encouraged to try new ideas, to extend their skills and knowledge.

4 Communications. How open and free are individuals in expressing feelings and opinions? Is there a free flow of information?

Members never express feelings, are secretive, and give few opinions. Information is hoarded and the flow impeded.	1 2 3 4 5 6 7	People are usually ready to give their views and feelings, and readily pass on information.

5 Rewards. The extent to which people feel they are rewarded for effort and recognized for good work rather than blamed or punished when things go wrong.

People are usually ignored but then blamed and criticized when things go wrong.	1 2 3 4 5 6 7	People are recognized for good work and rewarded for effort and creativity.

6 Conformity to norms. The extent to which people are expected to conform to rules, regulations, policies and procedures rather than being given the responsibility to do their work as they think best.

207

People conform to laid-down rules and standards at all times. Little personal responsibility is given or taken.	1 2 3 4 5 6 7	People do their work as they see fit; there is a great emphasis upon personal responsibility in the organization.

7 *Value placed on ideas*. How much are the ideas, opinions and suggestions of people sought out, encouraged and valued?

People are 'not paid to think'; ideas are not valued.	1 2 3 4 5 6 7	Efforts are made to encourage people to put their ideas forward. There is a feeling that the future depends upon people's ideas.

8 *Practical help available*. The extent to which people are ready to help each other by lending a hand, offering skills, knowledge or support.

People don't help each other; unwillingness to pool or share resources.	1 2 3 4 5 6 7	People are very willing and helpful to each other; pleasure is taken in the success of others.

9 *Warmth and support*. The extent to which friendliness is considered important in the organization and the extent to which people support, trust and like one another.

There is little warmth and support; this is a cold and isolating place to work.	1 2 3 4 5 6 7	This is a warm and friendly place; people enjoy coming to work. There is a belief in good relationships = good work.

10 Standards. The emphasis placed upon quality and standards and the extent to which members feel that challenging targets are set for themselves and for others.

Standards and quality are low; no one really cares very much.	1 2 3 4 5 6 7	Standards are high and challenging, members pick each other up and emphasize work quality.

Add up your score. If it comes to 30 or less, then you're working in a poor climate as far as managing yourself (and probably many other things) is concerned. There's not a lot to encourage self-managing efforts here.

If you scored between 30 and 50 then your organization has an average climate in terms of encouraging the growth of initiative-taking and personal responsibility for managing better.

Above 50 and you have a favourable climate for self-managing. With this sort of support you should be able to survive trouble, maintain yourself in good condition, and develop your skills and abilities beyond their present level in order to deal with new tasks and problems.

The total score may conceal big differences on some dimensions. Do your circled figures tend to one side or the other, or go down the middle (as one might predict in general climatic terms), or are they dispersed, revealing particular good and bad aspects? For example, your organization might have a very good climate with regard to standards and challenge (dimension 10) and yet be low on warmth and support and the amount of practical help which members are willing to give to each other (dimensions 8 and 9). Your department might be rich in physical resources (dimensions 1 and 2) and yet suffer from lack of encouragement to learn and little value being placed on ideas (dimensions 3 and 7). A good climate for self-managing contains support *and* challenge; resources *and* the freedom and encouragement to use them.

So what can you do if you're stuck in a poor organizational climate? Most of us should be able to take some steps towards managing ourselves where the climate supports and encourages us to offer ideas, help each other take initiatives and try out new approaches. But what happens in a poor climate where people are punished for not conforming to rules, where learning is not made much of a priority and where communications and standards are low?

In this situation there are the basic choices which we spelt out in Chapter 2:

- change the situation
- change yourself
- leave the situation
- put up with the situation

These are the logical possibilities even if they aren't easy! If you're stuck in a poor climate, try thinking about these, working through a mapping exercise (Chapter 2). Another obvious thing to try is the finding of friends, allies, contacts and comrades as detailed in Chapter 7. Just one friend or ally – even if you have to go outside the organization to get her or him – will transform your situation.

There are two major pressures for taking responsibility for managing yourself even in the most hostile or infertile climate. A practical reason for taking action stems from the consequences of not doing so. Consider the story of Derek:

> Derek had worked for twenty-nine years as a draughtsman with a large engineering concern until being made redundant in 1983. A retiring but clever child, his teachers had tried hard to persuade Derek's parents to let him stay on at school, promising a glittering professional career perhaps as an architect or designer. But Derek's parents were poor, had little education of their own and when the chance of an apprenticeship came up they pushed the fifteen-year-old out into the job. Derek had enjoyed his job and proved a willing and loyal worker and, in time, a first-class draughtsman. In many ways the job suited him down to the ground; technically demanding and calling for meticulous work to high standards, it usually meant that Derek worked alone, often working through breaks or staying after hours to finish the job. Derek liked his work, cared little about promotion and concentrated on providing for his family.
>
> When redundancy came it hit Derek hard. He went into a state of shock and moped around the house. After a year, his wife Sheila, needing the money and fed up with Derek, got herself a job and discovered a whole new world. Some of Derek's pals tried to encourage him to look for work and, later, to try voluntary work. But Derek knew he stood no chance of finding work. He felt useless and hopeless. Meeting and getting on with people had never been his strong suit. He felt awkward talking on the telephone and hated having to ask people for information. Socially he'd been content to let Sheila do the organizing. His job had encouraged his natural leanings to be shy and self-absorbed. Nothing in his work experience had prepared him for finding new work at forty-four. He had never learned to take initiatives and choose his own work, preferring to work to instruction. He had developed few skills with people and he had little curiosity or knowledge about the wider world outside his close job environment.

The story of Derek is a modern parable. Many hard-working, conscientious men and women have suffered similar fates and

211

, experiences over the last few years. Their work has not helped them develop the skills and capacities which are needed to find new work, turn to new methods, learn new trades and work with new people. In terms of the model shown in Chapter 3 (Table 3.2), they are stuck in stage/mode 2.

The work that we do forms us in certain ways – or *de*forms us. Through it we can develop capacities and abilities to high standards. We may become highly specialized with expertise of a high order but in a narrow field. Twenty or thirty years on and the situation can change out of all recognition – the foundry worker and the comptometer operator alike find their hard-won skills are obsolete and unwanted.

We sometimes hear that a decline in the 'work ethic' is the root cause of some of our modern industrial ills. Yet people like Derek have been faithful servers of this ethic and much good has it done them. Their children are not likely to make the same mistake. The work ethic needs to be replaced by a self-managing ethic. So long as organizations solve their crises through redundancies, they clearly can't be relied on to look after their employees, who must look to their own resources. While working, time and energy also has to be invested in maintaining knowledge and learning new skills. The generalized ability to learn how to learn has to be exercised and kept in trim. The most sobering aspect of Derek's story is that of the bright and able child rendered incurious, lacking in basic social skills, with a great future put behind him by the experience of thirty years of unchanging and, in this sense therefore, undemanding work. Professional workers, far from being immune to these dangers of stuckness and decay, are just as much at risk from deforming work. Pernickety accountants, methodical engineers, earnest teachers are both highly skilled and, in other ways, disabled, stuck in certain grooves of practice that can't be altered.

'Professional deformation' stems from organizational needs and demands for highly specialized and narrow professionalism (individual mode 2) in organizational stages 3 and 4 – the expanding and the established organization. As organizations pass through

212

these phases and begin to loosen up and relax this demarcation and extreme division of labour, those professionals who succeeded most under the old conditions find themselves stuck high and dry and eventually outside the organization unless they can learn and develop in accordance with the needs of the time.

This is the practical argument for striving to manage yourself even within the poorest, most hostile organizational climate. It is a matter of self-preservation, of maintaining the precious ability to continue learning.

The second pressure for keeping going, whatever the conditions, is quite a different one and less easy to describe. Simply it is the sense of a moral duty to look after, maintain and develop ourselves – not only for our own sake but for that of all humankind. The 'impossible situation' is especially one in which ideas must be kept alive so that there are seeds to be sown when conditions change. Seeds are kept alive in the example and practice of people who have the courage to 'keep keeping on' when the going is difficult. In this sense many of us feel that we have a duty to make the best of ourselves and to make a contribution to the general good. In religious terms this would be described as seeking to live the good life. T. S. Eliot's famous words give the flavour of struggle:

> And what there is to conquer
> By strength and submission, has already been discovered
> Once or twice, or several times, by men whom one cannot hope
> To emulate – but there is no competition –
> There is only the fight to recover what has been lost
> And found and lost again and again: and now under conditions
> That seem unpropitious. But perhaps neither gain nor loss.
> For us there is only the trying. The rest is not our business.

Although we live in an age that leans to science as its religion, the spiritual teachings are there for those who can hear them. When the Buddha taught that the path of human development led from suffering to enlightenment, he was describing a path for all human beings to tread. The conditions of the world which weigh upon us, the stuckness and triviality and absurdity we feel in our lives, our jobs, our organizations, are this suffering. It is a suffering we can only avoid at the cost of unawareness. Seen from this standpoint 'managing yourself' serves the higher purpose to make the best of ourselves, for ourselves, for others and for the force of good in the world.

This last point strikes a deeper tone than most of the book and, indeed, it is difficult to make without seeming to enlist the services of the Almighty in its marketing. But our urge to development, to awareness, conscious self-management, is not just a practical, sensible thing; it is fuelled by deeper drives which we can attempt to describe in psychological language as a 'need to know' or in traditional spiritual terms as a will to do The Good.

SPOTTING THE OPENINGS

In some ways managing yourself is like running your own small business. Keeping going requires an ability to spot openings and opportunities and keeping up the motivation to grasp them and make something of them. After years of running along defined channels we lose sight all too easily of the various openings for self-managing which abound in all organizations. There is a trick of seeing what's on offer which can help you survive, maintain or develop yourself.

What is the organization anyway? Do we believe in the single and reassuring structure of the organization chart, or is the organization like a kaleidoscope, reflecting different faces from different angles? When we talk of this thing we call *the* organization, we confer upon it a sense of solid identity which perhaps only exists because we refer to it in this way. There is a word for this – reification. We reify something when we treat an abstraction as if it were a real thing. When we believe in the map rather than the terrain we're standing on, we are doing just the same thing as when we start to call a collection of people *the organization* with needs, goals, structures, a culture and so on. We do this all the time of course for convenience, as we have in this book, yet really it is people who have goals, needs, motivation etc., not organizations. This is an important truth for the self-manager to grasp because we so easily hamstring ourselves by giving all sorts of powers and qualities to *the organization*. We tend to blame 'the system' for what is actually maintained by the activities of individuals including ourselves.

In this sense you can't work with an organization or group but only with people. Each person has a different picture of what the organization is, what its goals and purposes are, where the power lies, what values are important, and so on. These pictures are all different because *we* are all different and because we occupy different positions or vantage points. As we've just said, this view of the organization is like looking into a kaleidoscope – no fixed picture, but a lot of different patterns linked by various threads. Realizing that your view of the organization is only one of many alternative pictures that exist is the starting point for finding openings. Assuming a single view creates a prison – no wonder we complain we are stuck in the system – while opening up to other perceptions creates lots of gaps, loose ends and starting points.

Table 8.2 lists some resources, processes and structures which can be found in organizations. Some are better off than others, of course, but looking down this list, note which of these you participate in or take advantage of, those you neglect, and those you don't know about.

Table 8.2 Some organizational structures, activities and processes which may offer openings for managing yourself

	I use this a lot	I don't use this much	I don't know about this
Resources and materials			
1 Books, bibliographies, reviews, databases			
2 Journals, reports, papers			
3 Newsletters, brochures			
4 Packages			
5 Films, videos, audio			
6 Computers and programs			
7 Rooms, space, equipment			
8			
9			
10			
Activities and processes			
11 Training courses			
12 Coaching, counselling			
13 Job change, transfers, rotation, secondment			
14 Visits			
15 Appraisal interviews			
16 Consultants, visitors			
17 Conferences			
18			
19			
20			
Structures			
21 Working parties, project teams			
22 Teamwork meetings			
23 Committees, e.g. health and safety, productivity, welfare, etc.			

24 Quality circles
25 Workplace discussion
   groups
26 Trade unions, staff
   associations
27 'Think tanks'
28 Professional associa-
   tions
29 Luncheon clubs
30
31
32

There are some gaps in the table so that you can add any ideas you might have for further openings in *your* organization as you work through. You may find that you don't know a lot about what's available and in this case you will need to conduct an audit of resources and openings. The poorer your organizational climate, the fewer openings you will find, but you will most certainly discover some that you are not currently using well if you do a thorough audit. Asking other people, 'What do you do to find out about things here?' or 'What goes on here that I could get in on and learn from or get support from?' would be a good approach to starting your audit.

Having found some openings, pick one or two and get started. Do this on the basis of what you feel attracted to and don't worry too much about logic. Any effort at managing yourself needs energy or motivation first; the warmth has to come before the light. When you get the first inkling of a new idea you can nurture it, warm it up by thinking about it, talking about it and sometimes this may take quite a long time. Then, when you're ready you take the first steps on bringing the idea to light in some activity and this is the process of self-managing. Creating hot spots or pools of warmth for new ways of doing things, in ourselves first of all and then wider spreading into teams and departments, warming up the organization. This huge and cold abstraction again – 'the organization' – this is not our concern; we start with ourselves, warm ourselves up, get started and let the rest follow. If we wait on the organization and for others to act, we will wait for ever to cultivate our gardens.

9 The most important things about managing myself

The Most Important Things about Managing Myself

The Most Important Things about Managing Myself

The Most Important Things about Managing Myself

10 Sources and resources

This chapter provides a few starting points to take you further in your self-development. Most of it is a guide to further reading and there are some useful addresses at the end. Committing yourself to your own development brings home a number of realizations – not least that you have started something which will continue throughout life. If this book has whetted your appetite, we hope that you find some useful jumping off points here.

The following books are grouped under three headings:

- managing *self*
- managing *others*
- managing *organizations*

Each book is briefly annotated and is chosen to take you on from the various sections of *Managing Yourself*. Most of these books appeared previously in a list prepared by Vivien Whitaker and other staff at the Sheffield Business School for a Personal Development Programme for Training Agency Managers.

MANAGING SELF

Tom Boydell, *Management Self-development: A Guide for Managers, Organizations and Institutions*, International Labour Office, Geneva, 1985.
Contains 27 methods for self-development together with advice on how to promote self-development in the organization.

Sources and Resources

Tony Buzan, *Use Your Head*, Ariel Books, 1974.
Explains the latest discoveries about the brain and helps you to understand more clearly how your mind works. Includes tests and exercises designed to improve your reading power and memory, helping you to study more effectively, solve problems more readily and develop your own ways of thinking.

Roger Fisher and William Ory, *Getting to Yes*, Hutchinson, 1984.
The authors present a straightforward strategy for firmly pursuing your own interest while maintaining good human relations with those whose interests conflict with yours.

Dave Francis, *Managing Your Own Career*, Fontana/The Successful Manager Series, 1985.
Aimed at those seeking to get the most out of their working lives, between jobs or at a turning point in their careers, this book makes a structured investigation into personal needs, motives, talents and will help you adopt managerial techniques to progress in building your career and thereby to improve the quality of your work life.

Sally Garratt, *Manage your Time*, Fontana/The Successful Manager Series, 1985.
The effective use of time and delegation – when to delegate and to whom. Every area of time management is examined using 'real life' examples, from the telephone and the 'open door' to the diary and dictation.

Richard Hargreaves, *Starting a Business*, Heinemann, 1983.
A practical guide written by someone who has started his own business. As a simple introduction for new business people, with realistic advice and practical guidance, it will help anyone who wants to get a clearer understanding of business.

Barrie Hopson and Mike Scally, *Build Yor Own Rainbow*, Lifeskills Associates, 1984.
A workbook for career of life management which includes a range of exercises and questionnaires.

Andrew Kakabadse, Ron Ludlow and Susan Vinnicombe, *Working in Organizations*, Penguin, 1988.
The authors address 12 questions:
1 What is a manager's job all about?
2 In a new job, what do I need to do well?
3 As a manager, what am I like?
4 How can I improve my relationships at work?
5 How can I get the best out of people?
6 What do I need to know to manage groups of people?
7 What does it mean to be a good leader?
8 How do things happen in an organization?
9 How can I make an impact in my organization?
10 Where is my organization going?
11 What sort of organization am I in?
12 How can I make my organization work better?

Mike Pedler, John Burgoyne and Tom Boydell, *A Manager's Guide to Self-development*, (2nd edn.), McGraw-Hill, 1987.
Based upon a model of nine qualities of effective managers, this book provides diagnostic instruments and self development exercises.

Idries Shah, *Learning How to Learn*, Penguin, 1988.
An exploration of our own behaviour and that of our organizations and cultures in terms of classic *sufi* writings. A challenging and thought-provoking book.

R. Skynner and J. Cleese, *Families and How to Survive Them*, Methuen, 1985.
An amusing, easy-to-read book which explains how we relate to each other. A good synopsis of the major psychological theories.

David D. Stubbs, *How to Use Assertiveness at Work*, Gower, 1985.
To accomplish their objectives managers must work through others and they therefore depend on good relations and effective communications. David Stubbs draws on his experience as an assertiveness trainer to explain the relevant concepts and skills and shows how to apply them to particular problems, such as giving reprimands or resolving disputes.

MANAGING OTHERS

Margaret Attwood, *Developing Equal Opportunity at Work*, Occasional Paper: Employment Relations Resource Centre, 1986.
A very helpful practical guide.

David Clutterbuck, *Everyone Needs a Mentor*, IPM, 1985.
This book discusses mentoring as an alternative method of career development. It covers mentoring, and its associated benefits to the individual and the company, in a highly readable form.

David Clutterbuck and Marion Devine, (eds) *Businesswoman Present and Future*, Macmillan, 1987.
A series of articles which examine constraints, opportunities and innovative approaches relating to women in the work environment.

Steve Cooke and Nigel Slack, *Making Management Decisions*, Prentice Hall, 1984.
A broad, general guide to decision making in organizations, covering both technical and human aspects.

J.A. Dukes, *Assessing Management People: A Practical Guide*, Routledge and Kegan Paul, 1988.
A practical book looking at research findings and helpfully reviewing assessment centres.

William G. Dyer, *Team Building Issues and Alternatives*, Addison Wesley, 1987.
This book contains practical ways to implement and build a productive team. Special issues and problems in team building are also addressed.

John Harvey Jones, *Making It Happen – Reflection on Leadership*, Collins, 1988.
A radical and refreshing philosophy of leadership, with a proven track record – the author's reflections after 30 years at ICI.

John Kenney and Margaret Reid, *Training Interventions*, IPM, 1986.
This books gives an overview of the main issues in training and contains many useful references for those wishing to study aspects in more depth.

A. Mant, *Leaders We Deserve*, Martin Robertson, 1983.
An analysis of what makes a leader tick . . . and get elected. The author hopes this will be the most irritating book you have ever read.

Charles Margerison, *Influencing Organizational Change*, IPM, 1978.
This book is an easy-to-read, practical guide for those who wish to further their professionalism. In particular it shows how they can develop their skills to become effective in management and organizational development.

David Megginson and Tom Boydell, *A Manager's Guide to Coaching*, BACIE.
A practical guide to developing your own practices as a coach of your staff, and some ideas on developing coaching in the organization.

Mike Pedler, *Action Learning in Practice*, 1983.
A book of readings about practical applications of this method of management learning.

229

Sources and Resources

Ivan T. Robertson and Mike Smith, *Motivation and Job Design*, IPM, 1985.
The book aims to cover the major issues involved in the theory, research and practice of motivation and job design and also to present the material in a way that makes the book useful to practising managers.

MANAGING ORGANIZATIONS

D.A. Buchanan and A.A. Huczynski, *Organizational Behaviour – An Introductory Text*, Prentice Hall, 1985.
This is an excellent disussion of most of the relevant work on organizational behaviour. It examines such themes as the individual in the organization, groups, technology and management in a well-written manner.

W. Warner Burke, *Organization Development*, Addison-Wesley, 1987.
This book outlines a number of theories and models which are useful in diagnosing current organizational issues to assist in planning HRD and change strategies.

W.E. Deming, *Out of the Crisis*, Cambridge University Press, 1986.
The most radical of the quality gurus recognizing not only the basic principles such as negotiating customer–supplier needs, measurement, continuous improvement, etc., but also emphasizing that total quality requires fundamental shifts in the way we manage and organize.

Peter Drucker, The Coming of the New Organization, *Harvard Business Review,* January-February 1988.
An excellent article examining the possible effects of information technology on organizational structure and behaviour in the future.

K.B. Everard and Geoffrey Morris, *Effective School Management*, Harper & Row, 1985.
Deals with basic issues in school management – managing people, managing the organization, and managing change – with the aim of improving competence and performance. The book is extensively illustrated with examples of effective management and successful organization, and users are encouraged to interact with the material by working through the exercises and questionnaires.

Bob Garratt, *The Learning Organization*, Gower, 1989.
The author proposes as theory of organizations as 'learning systems', in which success depends on two key skills – learning continuously and giving direction. Strategies for developing these skills are then outlined.

Charles Handy, *The Future of Work*, Basil Blackwell, 1984.
Charles Handy thinks that there can be no return to old-style full employment, but he believes this provides the opportunity for a welcome diversification of work. His scenarios envisage what he calls 'flexilives' in which the formal job plays a smaller part, leaving people with more discretionary time and giving a new status to unpaid work, part-time work and scope for the self-employed. A thorough, persuasive and readable study of alternative options for work in an age of transition.

Charles Handy, *Understanding Organizations*, Penguin Business Library, 1985.
Handy looks first at seven concepts or frameworks which give a better understanding of people and organizations; motivation, roles, leadership, power, groups, organizational culture, politics. He then applied the concepts to current organizational issues, the development of people, work design, organizational systems and managment, and looks at future organizations. The book has a strong theoretical base but it is very readable. It contains excellent references and a guide to further study for each concept and application.

231

Sources and Resources

Charles Handy, *Understanding Voluntary Organizations*, Penguin Books, 1988.

Applying many of the theories put forward in *Understanding Organizations* the author discusses the ways in which non-profit making groups can function most efficiently.

Donald F. Harvey and Donald R. Brown, *An Experiential Approach to Organization Development*, Prentice Hall, 1988.

A useful book for anyone considering 'third party' interventions into organizations which examines every aspect of organization developments, including the intervention process and the challenge for OD in the future.

Jeff Hearn and Wendy Parkin, *'Sex' at 'Work'* – the Power and Paradox of Organization Sexuality, Wheatsheaf, 1987.

Reviewed as 'post-feminist' this work redefines concepts such as 'public', 'private', 'personal' and 'organizational' with respect to sexuality. It is constructively critical or previous theory and present practice.

John Hunt, *Managing People at Work*, Pan Books, 1984.

A fresh and practical approach to a subject that academics have often made difficult to follow. This book presents relevant ideas from the major areas of organizational behaviour: motivation, perception, communication, groups, notes, power, organizations, structures, managers, leaders, participation, change. Those theories and models which have endured because they have practical value are reviewed so that managers can decide for themselves whether behavioral tools can be useful and valuable to them. Highly readable.

Gerry Johnson and Kevan Scholes, *Exploring Corporate Strategy*, Prentice Hall, 1984.

A comprehensive book which looks at the underlying concepts, analytic methods and practical implications of corporate strategy. It considers decision making, the strategic environment, resources allocation, organizational structure, people and systems.

232

Ronnie Lessem, *The Roots of Excellence*, Fontana/The Successful Manager Series, 1985.
The book looks at the way companies develop and at the attributes of managers and organizations which lead to success. The text draws heavily on studies of four British organizations.

Ronnie Lessem, *Global Management*, Prentice Hall, 1988.
The author explains his vision of the new global order which perceives leaders as agents of change and managers as entrepreneurs and developers.

Management for the Future: How Leading International Companies Develop Managers to Achieve Their Vision, FME and Ashridge Management College, Berkhampstead, 1988.
Based on a survey of nine UK and European 'good practice' companies, with some useful lists of common cultural characteristics, transformational leadership characteristics and details of how organizations are changing.

G. Morgan, *Images of Organization*, Sage, 1980.
This book challenges our 'taken for granted' images of organizations and management and suggests a range of alternative metaphors to interpret organizational behaviour.

B. Moores (ed.), *Are They Being Served? Quality Consciousness in Service Industries*, Philip Alan, Oxford, 1986.
A fascinating collection of papers and cases across a variety of service organizations including British Rail, Thomas Cook, the NHS, Sainsburys, the Yorkshire Bank, libraries and others. The emphasis is on how to measure the service provided to the customer and many creative ways of doing this are highlighted.

Mike Pedler, John Burgoyne and Tom Boydell, *Applying Self Development in Organizations*, Prentice Hall, 1988.
This book illustrates the widespread applications and interest in self-development in commercial and public service organizations.

It provides creative ideas and designs for all those involved in management education and training.

Tom Peters, *Thriving on Chaos: A Handbook for a Management Revolution*, Macmillan, 1988.
Tom Peters' prescriptions for successfully responding to a rapidly changing environment – customer responsiveness, innovation, empowering people, learning to love change, building systems.

T.J. Peters and R.H. Waterman, *In Search of Excellence*, Harper and Row, 1982.
Provides theory and practical examples of organizations which have achieved, or are in pursuit of, corporate excellence. Gives examples of organizations which have been successful in establishing excellent relationships with employees and customers.

Edgar H. Schein, *Organizational Culture and Leadership*, Jossey-Bass, 1985.
This comprehensive text defines culture, examines how it begins and develops and how it can be changed.

Rosemary Stewart, *The Reality of Organisations*, Macmillan, 1985.
This book aims to help practising managers, seeking to help them diagnose what kinds of organizational problems they are dealing with and to understand the advantages and disadvantages of different ways of tackling them.

Peter Wickens, *The Road to Nissan*, Macmillan, 1987.
A personnel view of the establishment of the Nissan Factory in NE England which focuses on such issues as Quality Management, Ringi, Single Status, Role Negotiation, Cultures etc.

Sue Wood (ed.), *Continuous Development: The Path to Improved Performance*, IPM, 1988.
Lots of case studies of organizations in the UK.

SOME USEFUL ADDRESSES

American Society for Training and Development (ASTD)
Suite 305,
600 Maryland Avenue,
Washington DC 20024
USA

202 484 2390

The North American Society for Training and Development

Association of Management Education and Development
(AMED)
Premier House,
77, Oxford St.,
London W1R 1RB

01 439 1188

The professional association for management educators and
developers in the UK and abroad, with some 1500 members.

British Institute of Management (BIM)
Management House,
Cottingham Rd.,
Corby,
Northants NN17 1TT

0536 204222

The largest association for managers in the UK, with some
80,000 members.

European Foundation for Management Education (EFMD)
40 Rue Washington,
B-1050 Brussels,
BELGIUM

(2) 648 0385

The European professional association for management
education.

Institute of Personal Management (IPM)
IPM House,
Camp Rd.,
Wimbledon,
London SW19 4UW

01 946 9100

The professional association for personnel and human resources
practitioners in the UK, with some 20,000 members.

Women and Training Group
Hewmar House,
120 London Rd.,
Gloucester GL1 3PL

0452 309330

A women's training network offering a newsletter, courses,
regional groups.

 For a fuller list of institutions and colleges providing
management education services consult the *Management Training
Directory 1988/89* (9th ed.) published by TFPL Publishing, 22
St. Peters Lane, LONDON EC1M 6DS (01 251 5522).

236